Colonial America

Colonial America

Richard Steins

RAINTREE
STECK-VAUGHN
PUBLISHERS

A Harcourt Company

Austin · New York
www.steck-vaughn.com

Published by Raintree Steck-Vaughn Publishers, an imprint of Steck-Vaughn Company

Developed by Discovery Books
Editor: Sabrina Crewe
Designer: Sabine Beaupré
Maps: Stefan Chabluk

Raintree Steck-Vaughn Publishers Staff
Publishing Director: Walter Kossmann
Project Manager: Joyce Spicer
Editor: Shirley Shalit
Electronic Production: Scott Melcer

Consultant Andrew Frank, California State University, Los Angeles

Library of Congress Cataloging-in-Publication Data
Steins, Richard.
    Colonial America / Richard Steins.
        p.   cm. -- (The making of America)
    Includes bibliographical references and index.
    Summary: Describes the daily life and important events in the American colonies during the time of British rule.
    ISBN: 0–8172–5701-2
        1. United States — History — Colonial period, ca. 1600-1775 — Juvenile literature.
    2. United States — Social life and customs — To 1775 — Juvenile literature.   [1. United States —
    History — Colonial period, ca. 1600-1775.   2. United States — Social life and customs — To 1775.]
    I. Title. II. Making of America (Austin, Tex.)
    E188.S85   2000
    973.2—dc 21
                                          99–055983
Printed and bound in the United States of America
1 2 3 4 5 6 7 8 9 0 IP 04 03 02 01 00 99

Acknowledgments
Cover North Wind Picture Archives; pp. 7, 11 Corbis; pp. 12, 14, 16 The Granger Collection; p. 18 Corbis; p. 21 The Granger Collection; pp. 22, 24 Corbis; p. 25 The Granger Collection; p. 26 Corbis; pp. 27, 30, 32 The Granger Collection; pp. 33, 34, 36, 38, 39 Corbis; p. 40 The Granger Collection; pp. 41, 44, 46 Corbis; pp. 48, 49 The Granger Collection; p. 51 Corbis; p. 52 The Granger Collection; p. 54 Corbis; pp. 55, 61 The Granger Collection; p. 62 Corbis; pp. 63, 67, 68 The Granger Collection; pp. 70, 71, 72, 74, 75, 77 Corbis; pp. 79, 80 The Granger Collection; pp. 82, 85 Corbis.

Cover illustration: This colored engraving from the late 1800s shows the waterfront and harbor of Boston, Massachusetts, as it looked in the 1660s.

Contents

Introduction

I n 1782, Michel Crèvecoeur, a Frenchman who lived and farmed for many years in Orange County, New York, published a book entitled *Letters from an American Farmer*. In one of his most memorable passages, he asked the question "What attachment can a poor European emigrant have for a country where he had nothing?" Crèvecoeur went on to ask, "What then is the American, this new man?" He pointed out that in America, "individuals of all nations are melted into a new race of men."

To Crèvecoeur, "Americans" meant the descendants of Europeans who had settled in the Americas in the years after 1500. But the story of who was an American is much more complicated than that. Before Europeans came to North America, Native American people had lived here for many thousands of years. And once white Europeans had settled in America, Africans were brought against their will. From the 1500s until the early 1800s, somewhere between 8 and 15 million Africans arrived in the Americas as slaves. The terrible story of slavery stretched over centuries and caused suffering and death for untold numbers. There were indeed "individuals of all nations," as Crèvecoeur wrote, but they were most certainly not yet melting into a "new race."

Out of this great movement of peoples emerged a new North America, one shaped by the meeting of Indian, European, and African cultures. This meeting was all too often marked by conflict. People were cruelly used for their labor, and millions were killed by diseases brought from Europe. But Europeans and Native Americans also exchanged material things and ideas. And as the colonies grew, trade between Europe and a new kind of American became an important part of colonial life.

Opposite page: Guns and horses were brought from Europe to North America in the 16th century. They changed the lives of Native Americans. The European demand for beaver fur led to trade between the white settlers and Indian fur trappers like the man in this painting by Frederic Remington.

European Colonies in North America

The Europeans who arrived in the early 1500s did not regard North and South America as places to live. They saw the vast regions as a source of wealth for themselves and their rulers in Europe. For many of the early Europeans in the Americas, these continents were there to plunder.

Settlements and Colonies

Eventually, however, Europeans began to settle in the Americas. Their early settlements grew into colonies.

The early settlers were not equipped to handle the challenging environment of North America. It appeared to them to be a wilderness, even though Native American peoples had lived there for centuries. The Indians were sometimes welcoming and helpful and other times not. Many of the survival skills learned by the settlers were taught to them by Native Americans.

After several unsuccessful attempts, European nations established footholds in North America. The Spanish settled in the Caribbean area, Mexico, the American Southwest, and along the Pacific coast. They also built several small communities in what is now Florida and along the southeastern coast of the present-day United States.

The English built thriving communities in the Chesapeake Bay region. Religious groups from England settled in what is now Massachusetts. The Dutch founded communities in the area of New York State. The French explored and settled areas of Canada and the Mississippi River valley as far south as present-day Louisiana.

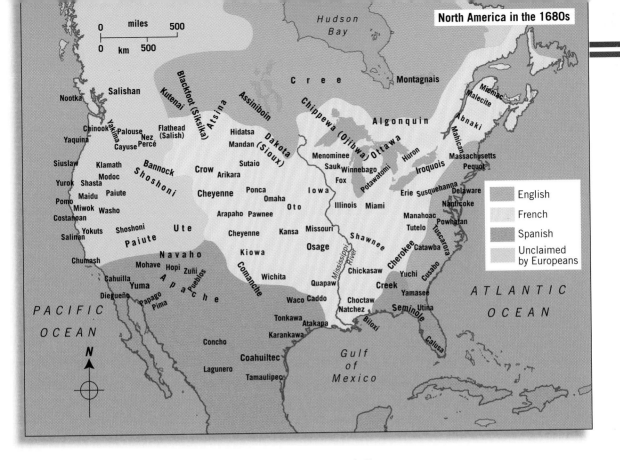

Hudson Bay

Nootka
Salishan
Kutenai
Blackfoot (Siksika)
Atsina
Assiniboin
Cree
Montagnais
Micmac
Malecite

Chinook
Yakima
Palouse
Flathead (Salish)
Nez Percé
Cayuse
Hidatsa
Mandan (Sioux)
Dakota (Sioux)
Chippewa (Ojibwa)
Ottawa
Algonquin
Abnaki
Mahican

Yaquina
Siuslaw
Klamath
Modoc
Bannock
Shoshoni
Crow
Sutaio
Arikara
Menominee
Sauk
Winnebago
Fox
Huron
Iroquois
Massachusetts
Pequot

Yurok
Shasta
Maidu
Paiute
Cheyenne
Ponca
Omaha
Iowa
Erie
Susquehanna
Delaware

Pomo
Miwok
Washo
Arapaho
Pawnee
Oto
Illinois
Miami
Nanticoke

Costanoan
Yokuts
Shoshoni
Ute
Cheyenne
Kansa
Missouri
Manahoac
Tutelo
Powhatan

Saliman
Paiute
Kiowa
Osage
Shawnee
Catawba
Tuscarora

Chumash
Navaho
Comanche
Wichita
Quapaw
Chickasaw
Creek
Cherokee
Yuchi
Cusabo
Yamasee

Mohave
Hopi
Zuñi
Pueblos
Apache
Cahuilla
Yuma
Diegueño
Papago
Pima
Waco
Caddo
Choctaw
Natchez
Biloxi
Seminole
Utina
Calusa

Tonkawa
Atakapa
Karankawa
Concho
Coahuiltec
Lagunero
Tamaulipec

PACIFIC OCEAN

ATLANTIC OCEAN

Gulf of Mexico

Mississippi River

English
French
Spanish
Unclaimed by Europeans

N

miles 500
km 500

Settlements developed in different ways and for different reasons. But they all needed money and materials in order to succeed. Companies were formed in Europe so that rich people could invest in new settlements. The company leaders recruited people to move to North America by promising them the hope of land and the chance to live their lives as free people.

Many settlers, however, came as servants. Africans came as slaves, carried across the Atlantic Ocean by the thousands to work in the North American settlements.

The Spanish in the Southwest

Spanish conquerors invaded Mexico in the early 1500s and defeated the Aztec Indians and other local peoples. During the 1500s, the Spanish were drawn northward into the American Southwest. They had heard legends of rich cities that were supposed to be in the vast regions north of Mexico.

By the 1680s, Europeans had claimed large areas of North America for themselves. Their claims overlapped with the ancestral homelands of Native American peoples.

The native people of the Southwest were from cultures thousands of years old. Their towns and cities were built of stone and clay, and some lived in multi-storied dwellings. The Spaniards called these buildings "pueblos," and the name "Pueblo Indians" was applied to various peoples living in the region.

Relations between the Spanish and the Indians were often hostile. Missionaries who accompanied the Spanish explorers to the American Southwest hoped to convert the local Indians to their form of Christianity, Roman Catholicism. Some Indians did not object, as long as they could add the religion to the beliefs they already held. But the missionaries wanted total dedication to Christianity and sometimes used force to get it. The Spanish also exploited Indians for labor and were harsh masters. The native people rebelled violently in the late 1590s, and the Spanish decided to keep only a small presence in the area. In 1609, they founded Santa Fe as

Popé (c.1630–90)

Popé came from a group of Pueblo Indians called the Tewa. He was a shaman, the name for a Native American holy man or medicine man. He defied the Spanish by refusing to stop the practice of his traditional religion. He also preached independence to his people, saying they should return to their old way of life before the arrival of the Spanish.

In 1680, Popé organized a revolt against the Spanish. It was so successful that it drove the conquerors out of New Mexico and back to Texas. Popé then began a campaign to rid the area of any trace of the Spanish presence. Churches were burned and the Spanish language was forbidden. Because of Popé's leadership, the native peoples were able to reassert their power and culture.

During the 1680s, Popé's powers were challenged by some of his own people. His territory also became a target for Indian groups from outside, such as the Apaches. Their raids caused great damage and loss of life. Popé died in 1690, and in 1692 the Spanish took control of their old territory.

their capital of New Mexico, along with a military outpost and a few Catholic missions.

The conflict between the Spanish and the Native Americans worsened throughout the 1600s. The missionaries continued to try and wipe out the native religions, and the Spanish demands for labor grew more brutal. In 1680, the hostility erupted in the Pueblo Revolt. Under the leadership of Popé, a respected holy person, the Pueblo peoples successfully drove the Spanish out of New Mexico. Around 400 Spanish settlers and missionaries were killed. The Indians lost some 350 people in the attack on Santa Fe alone, but the Spanish were forced to retreat to El Paso, Texas.

Fearing acts of revenge, the Indians abandoned their more vulnerable villages for fortified towns. It was a while before the Spanish returned. But in 1692, with the help of some Pueblo Indians, the Spanish regained their authority in the area. A few Pueblo groups remained free of Spanish control, particularly the Hopi in the western parts of the region.

The Pueblo Revolt was the most successful and long-lasting Indian rebellion during the colonial period in North America. In the 1700s, there were occasional outbursts of warfare between Indians and white settlers in the Southwest. During this time, the land was increasingly developed. The Spanish built ranches and farms, and began mining.

The 1700s saw the growth of Spanish missions in present-day Arizona. Spaniards also explored along the coast of what is now California,

In the late 1700s, Franciscan missionaries came and built the first missions in California. The oldest building in San Francisco, California, is the Mission of San Francisco de Asis. It is usually known now as Mission Dolores and was completed in 1791.

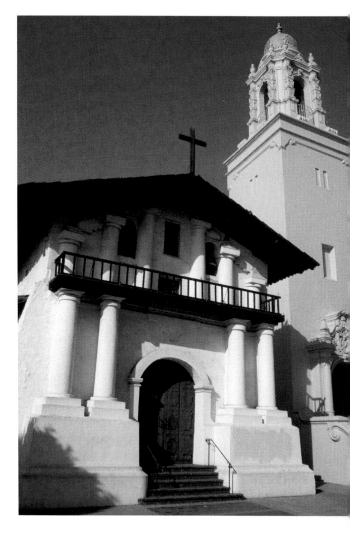

11

but settlement there proceeded slowly. The first "Californios," or Spanish settlers, grew crops and lived fairly free of control by the Spanish government.

Spanish Settlement in the American Southeast

The early Spanish colonies in the Caribbean area were not far from the mainland of North America. A number of Spanish adventurers had explored the Florida peninsula and claimed it for Spain. They gave the name "Florida" to a large area of the Southeast that now includes parts of Georgia and Alabama. The Spanish believed this would be a good place to build military outposts to protect the Spanish sea-lanes between Europe and the Americas.

The Spanish did not actually settle in Florida until they felt threatened by French interest in the region. In 1564, the

Sir Francis Drake, who was the first Englishman to sail around the world, was famous for his attacks on Spanish settlements. In June 1586, his fleet entered the harbor at St. Augustine. They attacked and burned the city before sailing back to England. This 1588 engraving shows the event.

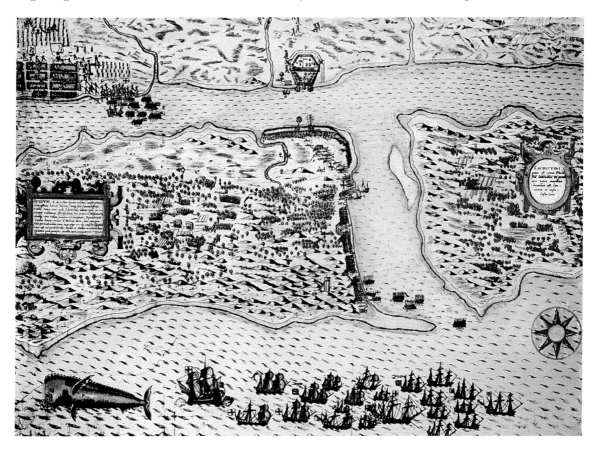

French established a fort near the mouth of the St. Johns River. The Spanish king, Philip II, ordered his military forces to expel the French, which they did with great brutality. The next year, the Spanish established St. Augustine, which is now the oldest permanent community in the United States.

In those early days, St. Augustine was not a city but more of an outpost. Most of its population were male soldiers. This region of Florida bordered English settlements to the north. It was therefore viewed as a Spanish threat, and was frequently attacked by the English during the next two centuries.

Florida was to be a contested area for years to come. It passed to the English in 1763, but was returned to Spain in 1783.

The land was of course inhabited by many Native Americans. It also became home to Africans from South Carolina. They sought to escape slavery by crossing into Spanish territory and living in Indian communities. Florida was swampy and heavily forested, which made it a good place to hide. In the early years, white settlements were nearly all built along the coastline. While the British colonies to the north grew in population, Florida remained undeveloped.

The French in the American South

During the 1500s and 1600s, French explorers and settlers established settlements along the St. Lawrence River in Canada. The French traded in beaver fur, and they built trading networks with Native Americans in Canada and the British colonies.

The French explorer René Robert Cavelier, Sieur de La Salle, traveled south along the Mississippi River valley. In 1682, he claimed the Mississippi River and all of its tributaries for France. He named this huge region Louisiana, in honor of the French king, Louis XIV.

Europeans first settled in Louisiana in 1699. The French Canadian explorer Pierre Le Moyne founded a settlement near what is now Biloxi, Mississippi. This town became the

In 1718, the French founded the city of New Orleans, on the coast of present-day Louisiana. This is a view of the settlement in 1719. New Orleans became Louisiana's capital in 1723.

center of government for Louisiana. In 1702, Le Moyne's brother Jean Baptiste Le Moyne was appointed governor. He moved the capital from Biloxi to Fort Louis on the Mobile River. The community was moved again to the site of present-day Mobile, Alabama, which became Louisiana's capital in 1710.

When communities had been established, French fur traders and missionaries began to explore the surrounding areas. In what is now the state of Louisiana, a settlement was founded in 1714. Named Natchitoches, it was at first a trading post and fortress designed to protect the Red River area from the Spanish in nearby Mexico and Florida.

The French government wanted to encourage settlers to migrate to Louisiana. In 1717, it granted control of Louisiana to the Company of the Indies, headed by the Scotsman John Law. The company advertised Louisiana as filled with gold and silver. But it was not, and the company soon went out of business. Nevertheless a huge number of settlers moved into the territory.

As whites settled in the region, they imported more and more African slaves. A series of laws known as the Code Noir (Black Code) was adopted in 1724. These controlled the lives and movement of slaves in the hope of preventing slave uprisings and protecting whites. Under the Code, slave owners were allowed to brand their slaves and cut off their ears if they ran away.

Relations between the French colonists and the native inhabitants were tense. Many of the early colonists traded with Native Americans for fur. But they also took over Indian territory for their plantations growing indigo, a plant for producing blue dye. When white settlers demanded that a group of Natchez Indians give up their sacred burial grounds, the Indians attacked Fort Rosalie, near what is now Natchez, Mississippi, in 1729. The 300 settlers were killed or taken prisoner. The French retaliated with the help of the Choctaw Indians, and almost completely wiped out the Natchez.

In the mid-1700s, thousands of Acadians migrated south from their homes in Nova Scotia. These people of French ancestry had refused to pledge loyalty to the British, who had ruled Nova Scotia since 1713. The French Acadians were expelled by the British in 1755. Many came to Louisiana because it already had a French population. They settled in the area that became known as the Cajun (from "Acadian") country.

Louisiana was almost impossible to defend because of its huge size. As a colony, it was never wealthy or densely settled. In 1762, the French gave the area west of the Mississippi River to Spain. After a period of resistance, the population accepted Spanish rule. Under the Spanish, the cultivation of rice and sugarcane was introduced into Louisiana. New Orleans prospered as a trade center and port.

Nova Scotia had originally been settled by the French in the early 1600s and named Acadia. British soldiers forcibly removed French Acadians from their homes in Nova Scotia and herded them onto ships. Many were taken to ports farther south, and eventually made their way to Louisiana.

British Colonial Society

To the east of Louisiana were 13 British colonies that hugged the Atlantic coast. In the north were Massachusetts, Connecticut, Rhode Island, and New Hampshire, which made up the colonies of New England. New York, New Jersey, Pennsylvania, and Delaware formed the Middle Colonies. South of these were Virginia and Maryland, known as the Chesapeake Colonies. The Southern Colonies comprised North Carolina, South Carolina, and Georgia.

From the early 1600s to the mid-1700s, the four regions developed societies that had differing ways of life and economies. In New England, for example, towns and small farms were more numerous than in the Chesapeake area, where farms were widely scattered and towns were scarce. Pennsylvania was founded as a colony by a religious group, the Quakers. Nearby Maryland, on the other hand, was supposed to be a haven for Roman Catholics. In the South, the economy was tied first to indentured servitude, then to slavery.

On the surface, therefore, the British colonies of North America seemed diverse. But by the 1760s, they had developed the first bonds of unity. This would allow the 13 colonies eventually to rebel against their mother country and form the new country of the United States.

The Colonial Legacy

All over the United States, you can see how different groups of Americans have left their mark on American societies today. Native Americans still struggle to keep alive a culture that was nearly destroyed by settlers from Europe. Strong African American communities exist in areas where African people were once brought as slaves.

British ways of governing still live on in our laws and government system. In the states that were once British colonies, other European countries have also left their imprint. The Dutch and Swedes had already settled in the Middle Colonies by the time the British took over.

The French influence is most noticeable in the South. The Cajun culture in Louisiana can be traced back to the 1700s, when French-speaking Acadians came from Nova Scotia. Africans also were forced to come in great numbers, and the blend of the two cultures can be seen today in New Orleans and other areas of Louisiana.

In the Southwest, the Native American and Hispanic people have lived together for hundreds of years. Their festivals and traditions often celebrate both cultures.

The Chesapeake Colonies

In 1606, King James I of England granted the Virginia Company the right to settle on lands in Virginia. His picture can be seen on their company seal. The Virginia Company was a joint stock company, which meant that people could buy a share in the new project. They did this hoping to make money when the new colony became successful.

The English colonies in North America began as a small number of settlements that had been established under difficult conditions. Unfamiliar terrain, cruel weather, and ignorance of how to survive in Indian lands made life almost unbearable for the early settlers.

Early English Settlements

The English made a number of failed attempts to establish colonies on the North American mainland. Their first successful settlements were along the shores of what are now Virginia and Maryland, on Chesapeake Bay. The very first of these was Jamestown, founded in 1606 by the Virginia Company of London. This company paid the costs of starting the settlement. In return, they were given control over the land and the chance of making money if the colony prospered.

Conditions in early Virginia were extremely harsh. Many settlers died of disease, and few knew what crops to plant or how to hunt or forage for food. The native people who lived in the region were not immediately hostile toward the new arrivals. But severe drought and the resulting food shortages caused conflicts. The settlers moved onto more and more Indian lands. A bloody outbreak in 1622 between Indians and colonists led to a change. The English rulers were not happy with the way the colony was being run, and in 1624 the Virginia Company lost its control. Virginia became a royal colony, governed on behalf of the English crown.

King James I (1603-1625) and his son and successor, Charles I (1625-1649), wanted profits from the colony, but they were not willing to spend money on the settlements. Even the governors they appointed to run Virginia had to be paid from taxes that were collected locally.

James I and Charles I did not think ordinary people should have a say in their government. They believed that kings had the right to rule given to them by God. But they allowed the settlers in Virginia their own assembly, called the House of Burgesses, which was founded in 1619. The royal governor would call on the House of Burgesses every time taxes were needed to pay for the cost of government.

In the 1650s, the assembly split into two "houses." The upper house was the Governor's Council, with members who were appointed by the governor and who served for life. The lower house, still called the House of Burgesses, was elected by the colony's male voters.

Early Chesapeake Society

The colonists in the Chesapeake region became growers of tobacco, which grew well in the soil of Virginia. Tobacco was in great demand in Europe, and it was exported in increasing amounts from Virginia.

To work the tobacco fields, Virginia farmers relied increasingly on a form of labor called indentured servitude. An indentured servant was usually a poor person from the British Isles, whose journey to North America was paid for in return for a period of unpaid labor. This period could last from four to seven years. After it was over, the indentured servant was free to follow his or her own life. For some people, becoming an indentured servant seemed like a good deal. In return for working in the tobacco fields or as a house servant, they had a chance to buy their own land and start a farm.

Medicine in the 1700s

Most people never saw a doctor in the early colonial days, and they were probably lucky that they didn't. Instead, amateur medicine was a necessary part of life in the 1700s. When colonists were sick, many relied on midwives, who delivered babies, and apothecaries, who made and sold medicines, for medical advice. A blacksmith was often consulted for the removal of a sty, maybe because the hot, steamy workplace helped draw out the infection.

Women provided most medical care in their own homes. They used Indian herbs and roots, and even professional doctors combined Indian remedies with European practices. As the century wore on, more and more professional doctors began setting up practices in cities. Hospitals were built, and medical standards were set. For country people, however, doctors remained beyond reach.

This might have been just as well, since medicine in the 1700s was severely limited. There was an understanding of infection, but treatments often killed patients instead of healing them. One of the worst medical practices was bloodletting. This was when a patient was deliberately made to bleed, in the belief that bleeding would remove illness from the body. Instead, sick people became weak, and the severely ill would bleed to death. The death of George Washington in 1799 was speeded up by just this method.

The Chesapeake society became one of masters and servants. A powerful minority of rich Chesapeake planters began to emerge in the 1600s. Many in this group were from English merchant families who traded with Virginia. They had migrated to North America themselves, and become planters. They were educated and ambitious and, by the 1670s, had taken control of the Governor's Council. These families obtained huge grants of land which they could pass on to future generations of their families. By the end of the century, the "first families" of Virginia dominated state politics.

Land Accumulation

A system known as headrights allowed people who were already wealthy to acquire large areas of land. Under this system, a person who paid for an immigrant to come from England was entitled to a plot of land, generally around 50 acres. People who could afford to do this accumulated a lot of property, and this led to an increase in the price of land. It became too expensive for people who had finished their indentured servitude and were ready to buy their own farm. The headrights system was abolished in the early 1700s. After that people had to buy land in the ordinary way.

Women and Families

Family life took a while to develop in the earliest settlements. This was because fewer women than men migrated to the Chesapeake area. As a result, many men in the settlements' early years went unmarried, or married later in life. The shortage of brides meant that women could pick and choose among husbands. Even poor servants sometimes married wealthy planters, who would buy out their indenture contracts from their employers.

Illness remained one of the major obstacles to family life in the Chesapeake settlements in the 1600s. Typhoid, malaria, and dysentery meant that, on average, people lived only until their mid-forties. Families often lost at least half of their children to disease. These high death rates were of course shattering to family life. The situation did not change much until the early 1700s. By this time, colonists were beginning to develop immunity to some diseases.

Few women lived at Jamestown during the first years of the settlement. In 1619, the Virginia Company sent the first group of women who were intended as wives for the settlers. Many were convicts who would otherwise have been sent to prison. Men who chose a bride had to pay the Virginia Company 120 pounds (54 kg) of tobacco to cover the cost of the woman's journey from England.

Cecil, the second Lord Baltimore (pictured here), became the proprietor of Maryland when his father died in 1632. He realized his father's dream of a colony for Catholics. He appointed his brother, Leonard Calvert, to be the first governor of Maryland. Cecil himself never visited the colony he founded.

Maryland

After the English government had made Virginia into a royal colony, it was free to give away the land as it wanted. In 1632, King Charles I awarded about 6.5 million acres of land, north of the Potomac River and east of Chesapeake Bay, to his friend Lord Baltimore. The new colony was named Maryland in honor of King Charles's wife, Queen Henrietta Maria.

Lord Baltimore was a Roman Catholic from the wealthy Calvert family. He intended to make Maryland a refuge for other Catholics. Catholics formed a minority of the British population, and many of them were, like Baltimore, rich. However, they were not permitted to worship in public and could not hold political office. A colony where they could practice their religion openly was appealing to many English Catholics.

Lord Baltimore died in 1632, before the settlement began. The charter passed to his son, Cecil, the second Lord Baltimore. As proprietor of the new colony, Baltimore was free of royal taxation and enjoyed wide powers to run the new settlement. In return, he allowed England to control the colony's foreign relations and trade. To attract Catholics to America, Baltimore offered wealthy fellow countrymen land grants, provided they brought over other settlers at their own cost. His plan was to transplant the English manorial system to Maryland. The manorial system was one in which peasants labored for a proprietor. The proprietor had his own courts of law and even a private chapel for worship.

Baltimore himself remained in England and governed from afar. Catholics, including many of Baltimore's Calvert relatives, received large grants of land. But from the

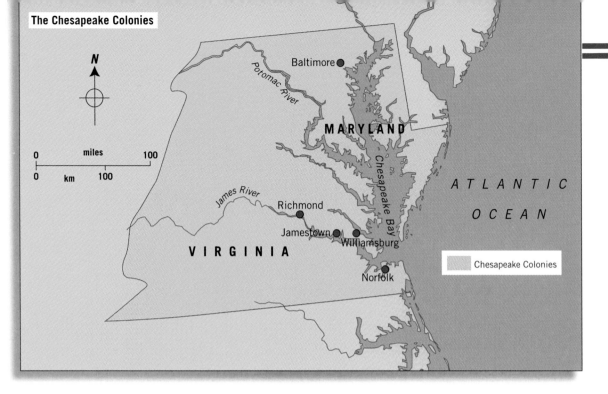

The Chesapeake Colonies

beginning, it was Protestants who formed a majority of the population. As a result, there was tension between Protestants and Catholics. The Catholics dominated the Maryland assembly's upper house and held high office in the colony. Protestants dominated the lower house.

In 1649, Lord Baltimore wrote the Act for Religious Tolerance, which was meant to guard the freedom of both Protestants and Catholics. However, in the 1650s, Protestants tried to bar Catholics from voting. This led to armed conflict, and Protestants controlled Maryland until 1658. Then the Calverts regained power, but their rule of the colony continued to be troubled by Protestant resistance.

Conflict in Chesapeake Society

Until the mid-1600s, the main divisions in Virginia and Maryland were between farmers and indentured servants. But this changed by the late 1600s, and even greater inequality began to emerge. One major cause was a drop in the price of tobacco. Cheap tobacco reduced the planters' profits. This in turn made it harder for servants to save enough money to buy land.

Together, Virginia and Maryland made up the Chesapeake Colonies. Settlements grew around Chesapeake Bay, and the tobacco industry expanded with the population.

The Declaration of the People, against Sr Wm Berkeley, and present Gobernor of Virginia

For, having upon specious Pretences of publick Works raised vnjust Taxes vpon the Commonaltie, For Advancing of Private Favourites And other sinister Ends, but noe visible Effect in any Measure adequate.

For having during the long time of his Government, in any Measure advanced this hopefull Colonie, either by fortifications, Townes, or Trade.

For, having abused, and rendered Contemptable, his Matie's Justice, by advancing to Places of Judicature, Scandalous and ignorant Favourites.

For having wronged his Matie's Prerogative, and Interest, by assuming the monopolie of the Bever Trade.

For having in that unjust Gaine betrayed and sold his Matie's Countrie and the Liberties of his Loyall Subjects to the Barbarous Heathen.

For having, Protected, favoured, and Emboldned, the Indians against his Matie's most Loyall Subjects; never Contriving, requiring, or appointing any due or proper Meanes of Satisfaction for theire many Incursions, Murthers, and Robberies, Committed, vpon Vs.

For having when the Armie of the English, was vpon the Tract of the Indians, which now in all Places, burne spoile, and Murder and when Wee might with ease, have destroyed them, who were in open hostilitie.

For having expresslie, countermanded, and sent back, our Armie by Passing his word, for the Peaceable demeanours of the said Indians, who Immediatly prosecuted theire Evill Intentions Committing horrid Murders and Robberies, in all Places, being Protected by the said Engagement and Word passed by Him the said Sr Wm Berkeley having Ruined and made Desolate a greate Part of his Matie's Countrie, having now drawn Themselves into such obscure and remote places, and are by theire Successe see Emboldned, and Confirmed, and by theire Confederates Strenghned That the Cryes of Blood, are in all Places, and the Terror and Consternation, of the People see greate, That They are not only become difficult but a very formidable Enemie Who might with ease have bin destroyd.

In 1676, the people of Virginia were unhappy with their governor, William Berkeley. This "Declaration of the People" listed their complaints. As well as protesting against taxes, the document said that the governor had done little to improve the colony. It also accused him of favoring the Indian population over the white settlers.

The number of landless people in both colonies grew, creating a larger gap between the planters and those without land. Both groups became suspicious of each other, with planters fearing the landless people as "rabble," and the poor regarding planters as "greedy."

Before the 1670s, most free white men could vote. In 1670, however, the Virginia House of Burgesses limited voting rights to male heads of households. They believed that only those with property had the right to vote on the colony's policies and future. This change shows how class distinctions had grown in Chesapeake society. It led to tensions that would sometimes erupt in servant rebellions and in major political crises.

Bacon's Rebellion

The most serious political crisis in the Chesapeake occurred in 1676. It has come to be known as Bacon's Rebellion. By the mid-1600s, frontier settlers were continually moving onto Indian lands. The government in Virginia wanted to keep peace with the Indians to protect trading relations. The settlers, however, wanted the government to do more to protect them against the Indians whose lands they were taking. This was one reason for the rebellion.

There were also other, deeper reasons. High taxes, low tobacco prices, and resentment against the rich were at the root of the uprising. The frontier people aimed their complaints not only at the Indians, but at the government in Jamestown and the richest planters. Poorer planters and farmers formed the backbone of the protest, which was led by a man named Nathaniel Bacon.

Bacon was hardly a poor man, but he saw himself as one of the frontiersmen and the "outsiders." These were people who did not run the government and were not part of the upper levels of society.

Bacon was a threat to the rulers of colonial Virginia. In addition to fighting Indians, he made raids on plantations belonging to government supporters. In June 1676, Bacon led 500 men into Jamestown, where he forced the governor and the House of Burgesses to accept reforms in the way they ran the colony. Bacon's control of the colony was short-lived, although many people supported his aims. The governor proclaimed Bacon a traitor. In September 1676, Bacon and his men marched on Jamestown and burned it to the ground.

Suddenly, in late October, Bacon died after a short illness. Forces arrived from England to help the colonial government fight the rebels. Support for Bacon's cause declined. Many of Bacon's followers were executed and the plantations of his wealthier followers were seized by the government.

Nathaniel Bacon (right) was a fairly wealthy plantation owner, but he led the protest against Virginia's privileged leaders. He is seen here confronting the governor, William Berkeley (left), who was in fact his cousin.

Bacon's Rebellion was a revolt of the many against the few, or against the "grandees" as Bacon called them. When the rebellion failed, some stability slowly returned to the Chesapeake colonies.

Slavery and Tobacco

Political stability was closely related to the price of tobacco. When prices were high, the colonists prospered. When they were low, there were problems and discontent in the Chesapeake area. A series of English laws starting in 1660 badly affected the tobacco industry. The Navigation Acts,

Digging Out Jamestown

Jamestown was the colonial capital of Virginia, but it was destroyed in Bacon's Rebellion and was only partially rebuilt. When the colonial capital was moved to Williamsburg in 1699, Jamestown fell into decay. In 1934, the National Park Service began to examine the site on which Jamestown had been established in 1607. Only an old church tower and a few gravestones could be seen.

The site of Jamestown has been re-created to show how the settlement appeared in the early 1600s. A copy of a colonial fort is in the grounds of the park, as are replicas of the three original ships that brought the white settlers to Virginia. An Indian village has been built in the way historians believe it looked during the 1600s. People in period costumes perform tasks and demonstrate crafts and skills of the time.

Digging continues at Jamestown, and in 1996, the remains of the original fort were discovered.

as they were called, said that certain goods must be shipped only to England or to other English colonies, such as those in the West Indies. The price of tobacco dropped greatly and the Chesapeake colonists suffered.

Stability was helped by the weakening of the servant system in the late 1600s. Fewer servants arrived because of improving economic conditions in England. The region began to use slave labor instead. This lessened the differences between poor whites and rich whites. Now the main difference was between whites and blacks.

During the 1690s, planters began importing slaves from the West Indies. Soon the majority of workers in the tobacco fields were African slaves rather than white servants.

As a work system, slavery seemed to make sense. Unlike servants, slaves did not become free after seven years. The children of slave mothers became slaves as well. Slavery, therefore, was a work force that could go on from one generation to the next. Unlike servants, slaves had no

"Be it therefore enacted that all Negroes, mulattoes, mestizoes or Indians, which at any time heretofore have been sold, or now are held or taken to be, or hereafter shall be bought and sold for slaves, are hereby declared slaves, and they, and their children, are hereby made and declared slaves."

Colonial law making slavery legal

This picture of a Virginia tobacco plantation was used as a tobacco label in the early 1700s. For some plantation owners, slavery meant huge profits and a life of luxury.

> "Slaves should be at their work as soon as it is light, work till it is dark, and be diligent while they are at it."
>
> *George Washington, first president of the United States of America*

political or economic rights. However slavery added a new instability to the region, as whites always lived in great fear of slave uprisings.

At first, most tobacco farms were relatively small. Tobacco planters in the Chesapeake had just a few slaves, with whom they worked side by side in the fields. This closeness meant slaves could be watched carefully. It was very different from slavery on a large sugar plantation in the West Indies.

The American colonies were all multicultural societies. But that meant different things in different colonies. In the Chesapeake region, differences were deeply rooted in racial divides, first between whites and Indians, and then between whites and blacks.

First Families of Virginia

By the end of the 1600s, members of several English merchant families controlled politics in Virginia. And they passed on their wealth and power to future generations, giving American society many distinguished figures.

An extraordinary number of Virginians have held the office of president of the United States. They include George Washington, Thomas Jefferson, James Madison, and James Monroe. Lesser known Virginia politicians also provided a link between colonial families and later generations in politics.

Among these families were the Byrds, the Harrisons, the Lees, and the Taylors, to name but a few. The Harrisons gave the country a pair of generals and U.S. presidents: William Henry Harrison, 9th president of the United States (1841) and his grandson, Benjamin Harrison, 23rd president (1889–93).

The Taylors also produced a president: Zachary Taylor, 12th president (1849–50). The Lees had many distinguished family members, including the great Civil War general, Robert E. Lee. One colonial-era family that persisted in politics well into the 20th century is that of the Byrds, whose members served as governors of Virginia and as U.S. senators.

Virginia politics have changed to the extent that an African American was elected governor in the 1980s. But the historic "first family" names can occasionally be heard in political campaigns to this day.

3

The New England Colonies

In the early 1600s, Englishmen began building settlements north of the Chesapeake, in the region of the United States now known as New England. These settlements grew into the colonies of Massachusetts, Connecticut, Rhode Island, and New Hampshire.

Unlike the Chesapeake region, New England was not good country in which to grow tobacco. The land, in fact, was hard and rocky and was unsuited to large-scale farming. As a result, New England developed a different economy and way of life.

Puritans in North America

Some of the first settlers in New England were Puritans from England. Although they were part of the Church of England, they didn't agree with the way their church was run. Their own beliefs were more strictly based on the Bible.

The first group of Puritans to settle in America came to be known as "the Pilgrims." They arrived in 1620 and settled in what is now Massachusetts. Their community, Plymouth, was governed under the Mayflower Compact. This was an agreement for self-government that they had made on the journey from England. After a difficult start in a bitter winter, and with the help of native inhabitants, the new settlement took root.

The Pilgrims were Separatist Puritans, which means that they had chosen to separate themselves from the Church of England. In 1630, another group of Puritans came to North America. These Puritans did not want to separate from their

The first Puritan families arrived in North America in 1620. They settled in an area that had until recently been the Indian village of Patuxet. The Indians had been wiped out by disease, and the Puritans also suffered hardship and fatal illness in their first year.

church, but to set an example for other Christians to follow. Their settlement in America would be like a "city on a hill" for all to see, one that would shine like a "beacon." (The name of Beacon Hill, an area in Boston, comes from this idea.) This group founded the Massachusetts Bay Colony near what is now the city of Boston. The Massachusetts Bay settlers also had very difficult early years.

Puritans arrived in families, unlike in the Chesapeake, where groups of men had come first. Also unlike Virginia and Maryland, New Englanders built many towns. By the mid-1600s, there were some 130 towns in the region.

As settlements grew into colonies, the growth of New England society became influenced more by economics than by Puritan religious beliefs. Commerce, trade, and agriculture dominated life in the northern colonies.

Relations with the Indians

As in other parts of North America, relations between the white settlers and Native Americans grew worse as time went on. The Puritans believed strongly that they were God's chosen people. They thought of the Indians as sinners, and that it was their duty to convert them to Christianity. The Puritans set up their own kind of missions, called "praying towns." They made it difficult for native peoples to practice their own religions and tribal traditions.

At times, the Puritans used violence against the Indians. During the 1630s, a group of Puritans attempted to settle in the Connecticut River valley on lands of the Pequot tribe. Several battles, known together as the Pequot War, took place over a period of a few years. The Pequot people raided white settlements, and the new settlers fought back. The war came to a violent end in 1637, when white forces from Connecticut and Massachusetts joined with Indian allies in a bloody attack on a Pequot village. They burned the village and killed more than 500 men, women, and children.

Even when there was no violence, Puritans crowded Native Americans out of their land. As settlers moved greater distances from the towns, they came into closer contact with

Native American Slaves

Africans were not the only people forced into slavery during the colonial period. Native Americans at times were also enslaved, although not in the enormous numbers that Africans were.

In the early 1700s, there was a brisk business in the importation of Native American slaves from the Carolinas to New England. The men were used as laborers, while women and children were forced to be house servants.

By 1715, three northern colonies had banned the importation of Indian slaves. Many of the slaves resisted their horrible new conditions. One white resident of New England complained that Indian slaves were "malicious, surly, and revengeful," and that they committed "conspiracies, insurrections, thefts, and other [terrible] crimes."

What to the white man was a "crime" was to a Native American the chance to defend himself and preserve his dignity as a human being. The importing of Indian slaves into New England declined during the early 1700s, but there were still many Indians employed as servants.

As white settlers expanded onto more and more land, whole areas of woodland vanished. This engraving of a farm of the 1700s shows the remaining tree stumps where the land has recently been cleared. With the woodland went the Indians' means of survival. Native Americans, such as the woman in the foreground paddling the canoe for her white master, were forced into working for settlers on land that was once theirs.

Indian lands. By clearing away forests for timber and fuel, the settlers changed the land in ways that damaged native life. Without forests, deer were no longer so readily available, and the wild plants used by Indian people for medicine and food could no longer grow. Settlers also had domestic livestock, which ran wild over Indian lands when they foraged for food. Pigs, for example, damaged cornfields and sites where shellfish were gathered.

Conflict between Indians and whites erupted again into open warfare in the 1670s. For years, the white settlers of Plymouth had been forcing the Wampanoag people off their ancestral homelands. Their leader, Metacom (who was named "King Philip" by white people) decided to fight back. He and his followers attacked 52 towns and killed more than 800 white people before the colony sought help. With the aid of Mohawk Indians and some of the praying towns, the colonists turned the attackers back. In 1676, Metacom was

hunted down and killed, and hundreds of other Indians were sold into slavery.

This conflict, known as King Philip's War, greatly reduced the Indian population of southern New England. It also made whites even more hostile toward Indians. A number of the praying towns were abandoned and even greater restrictions were put on tribal life.

Puritan Control

New England's many small towns were built along the coast or on rivers. The town was the center of community life for the Puritans. Each town had a church, a school, and the homes of the inhabitants. The church often also served as a meeting hall and was the geographic and social center of the community. It was usually a simple wooden structure with benches made of wood. This plain environment was exactly what Puritan religious leaders wanted: a place where the word of God could be concentrated on for five to six hours every Sunday. Town inhabitants were required to attend sermons on Sundays and sometimes on Thursdays.

King Philip's War erupted in 1675. Tribal leaders in the Massachusetts region tried to resist the colonists who took away their land and their authority. King Philip, or Metacom, of the Wampanoag was killed in 1676, and the war came to an end.

In Puritan communities, going to church was not a matter of choice. Sermons could be long and demanding. In 1675, Puritans in Massachusetts began locking churches during the service to stop their congregations from leaving.

Puritans thought of their church as a community of men and women who had entered an agreement with God and each other. They were influenced by Calvinism, the teachings of the French religious reformer John Calvin who had died in 1564. Calvinism taught that God chooses certain people to save, and the rest are forever sinners. As God's chosen people, the Puritans considered themselves "saints," and church members were expected to act as such. Church elders kept an eye on the behavior of everyone in town. People whose beliefs were different from those of the Puritans were often not accepted into the community.

Ministers were highly respected figures in the community, but they were not allowed to hold any government office. However, the Puritans had a special relationship with civil government. This relationship between Church and State was something that would be debated throughout the course of American history.

Puritans had no doubts that the government of their colonies should be in the service of Puritanism. The charter of the Massachusetts Bay Colony gave "freemen" the right to make laws and govern the colony. But freemen were restricted to male church members. Other men were called "inhabitants," and could not hold government positions. They were only allowed to take part in town meetings, where they could speak out and vote on local issues.

Distributing the Land

The town meeting had the important responsibility of distributing town land to settlers. Land throughout the colony was controlled by the General Court, which was the colony's governing body. The General Court gave plots of land to the town once the Indians had given up their claims on it. Usually they had been persuaded to trade land in return for manufactured tools and utensils.

Once in possession of the land, the founders of the town would divide it up among themselves and any newcomers who had been allowed to settle in the town. Each family would receive a lot large enough for a house and a garden. They would also receive one or more pieces of farmland on the edge of the town. With the houses grouped in the middle of the town, most people could walk from their homes to work in their fields. Wealthier people tended to get larger plots of land. Some land was reserved for common use such as grazing and timber, and some was reserved to be given later to newcomers.

Singing with More than One Voice

A historian has written of the Puritans that their people "sang with more than one voice." Puritans, like other people, had differing opinions about things, and disagreement was never far below the surface. Puritan leaders knew this, although they regarded it as wrong.

One young minister, Roger Williams, who had arrived from England in 1630, disturbed the Puritan elders with his open criticisms. Williams believed that government spoiled the purity of the Church, and that Church and State should be totally separate. To preserve purity, Williams also wanted only church members to be allowed to attend sermons.

Women Making Money

Colonial women in the 1700s were confined largely to the home. Their work was cooking, washing, and gardening, all of which tasks were considerably harder and more time-consuming than they are now. They also of course raised their children.

Many discovered as the century wore on that money could be made by selling produce from their gardens. By 1800, women kept gardens mainly to grow crops to sell in the market.

In New England, some African American women sold their produce and saved the money to purchase their freedom. New England women often grew onions and sold them. Almost all women who sold crops also made money from the sale of eggs, butter, cheese and salted or smoked meats. Indian women specialized in selling berries, herbs, and nuts.

This "egg money," as it was sometimes called, was used to buy goods, such as candles, needles and thread, or soap. It could buy other food and drink products which weren't made at home, such as sugar, rum, tea, or chocolate. By taking the results of their work into a wider market, women of the 1700s were able to earn extra money and achieve a small degree of economic independence.

A typical kitchen in a colonial American home.

His outspokenness resulted in Williams being banished in 1635. In what is now Rhode Island, he bought land from Narragansett Indians and founded the community of Providence. By 1643, there were three other settlements along Narragansett Bay: Portsmouth, Newport, and Warwick. People were coming to the new communities attracted by the promise of religious freedom. Jews, as non-Christians, were denied political rights in other colonies, and so Rhode Island was a welcome haven to them. The law there said that religion made no difference to a person's rights.

Roger Williams (c.1603–83)

Roger Williams was a minister, a believer in religious freedom, and a founder of Rhode Island Colony. He was born in England and graduated from Cambridge University in 1627. Williams became a Puritan early in his career.

In 1630, he migrated to Massachusetts Bay Colony, and by 1634 was a minister at the Salem church. Williams got in trouble with colonial authorities almost immediately. He especially alarmed Puritan leaders by saying that they had no authority over matters of conscience. In 1635, he was banished from the colony.

Williams journeyed south, where he founded a refuge for dissenters from Puritanism. He went to England to get a charter from Parliament for his settlement, which became the colony of Rhode Island.

Williams was unusual among white colonists because he questioned the right of settlers to take native lands. He prided himself on having good relations with the Indians and often tried to make peace with them. But he could not prevent the outbreak of King Philip's War, and even served with the militia against the Wampanoag people.

Throughout his life, he remained faithful to the ideal of religious liberty. As he got older, he separated himself from established churches, although he always thought of himself as a Christian. Even those who disagreed strongly with him usually liked Williams personally because of his kindness and honesty.

Roger Williams left the
Massachusetts Bay Colony
in disgrace. When he arrived
in present-day Rhode Island,
he was befriended by the
Narragansett people. It was
on their land that he founded
his settlement committed to
religious tolerance.

Another powerful dissenter in early New England was
Anne Hutchinson, an ardent Puritan. One of her strongest
beliefs was that people could be saved only by the grace of
God, not by any good works they did. That message greatly
alarmed John Winthrop, the governor of Massachusetts Bay
Colony. He believed that Hutchinson was undermining
order in the community, and had her tried and banished.
Along with Roger Williams, Anne Hutchinson's name has
come to stand for freedom of religion and conscience in
colonial America.

The Splintering of Puritanism

Other problems within Puritanism caused it to split often in
the 1600s. Disputes over church teachings and methods of
government led to the founding of Connecticut in the 1630s,
when Thomas Hooker and 800 colonists moved to the
Connecticut River valley and eventually founded the town of
Hartford. Hooker believed that "the people," not just church
members, should have a say in the community. But in

Anne Hutchinson (1591–1643)

Anne Hutchinson was born Anne Marbury in Lincolnshire, England. She was the daughter of a minister who had been imprisoned twice for preaching against the Church of England. Although Anne had no formal education, she learned by listening to her father talk about religion and government.

When Anne was 21, she married William Hutchinson, with whom she had 14 children. In addition to raising her growing family, Hutchinson became active in religious affairs. She was a strong follower of the preacher John Cotton. In 1633, Cotton was forced to leave England because of his Puritan sympathies. With Hutchinson's eldest son Edward, Cotton migrated to New England. The rest of the Hutchinson family followed in 1634.

Once settled in Massachusetts, Anne Hutchinson started weekly prayer meetings for women, and it was at these meetings that she first spoke against the teachings of ministers in her church. Hutchinson's beliefs in salvation through the grace of God gained support, and the civil and religious leaders saw her beliefs as a danger to their authority. She was brought to trial for heresy. At her trial, she defended herself brilliantly, but in the end she refused to deny her beliefs and was thrown out of the Church. She was banished from the colony in November 1637.

Anne and her family and friends moved to Rhode Island in 1638 and founded a new colony. After her husband died in 1642, Hutchinson took her younger children and settled in Pelham Bay in New York. They later moved to Long Island, and there, in 1643, she and most of her family were killed by Indians.

> "Quakers are malignant and assiduous promoters of doctrines directly tending to subvert both our church and state."
>
> *Massachusetts official on the Quakers*

practice, voting was still restricted to men who were heads of households, and mostly church members anyway. The Fundamental Orders of Connecticut, a kind of constitution, was adopted in 1639.

While these disputes went on, colonial society was changing in other ways. The population of New England was growing faster than church membership. People were becoming more interested in material things than in religion. Puritan communities still tried to enforce church rules in spite of what was happening. But people drifted away from the church, and different kinds of people moved into the colonies.

The changes in society may have seemed terrifying to the Puritan religious leaders. Fear of these changes sometimes led to extreme behavior. In Salem, Massachusetts, for example, a period of witch hunting gripped the community in 1692.

In the 1650s, Quakers began moving into Massachusetts. They believed that God spoke to each person individually. This was another threat to Puritan beliefs. A few Quakers who refused to leave were hanged.

By the early 1700s, however, Quakers were tolerated in Massachusetts, and had strong communities elsewhere in the

The Puritan leaders of Massachusetts distrusted anybody who did not follow their religion. When people of the Quaker faith began to settle in the colony, they were hounded and persecuted. Some were branded with hot irons and whipped as they were marched through Boston.

The Salem Witch Trials

Seventeenth-century people believed in witches, who they thought were possessed by the devil. They believed witches had supernatural powers to torment their neighbors and cause illness and death. In Massachusetts law, anyone convicted of witchcraft could be put to death.

Fear of witches became a consuming passion in Salem, Massachusetts, in 1692. Many people were accused of witchcraft, and 20 men and women were executed. Most of the accused were single women over the age of 40, while most of the accusers were young girls between the ages of 11 and 20 who claimed to have been "possessed" by witchcraft.

The panic got completely out of hand, and people began to question what they were doing. The governor of Massachusetts decided to put an end to all trials for witchcraft. Historians have argued about the causes that led to the Salem trials. While many different reasons have been put forth, there is no doubt that the turmoil took place against the backdrop of a society that was changing rapidly. In that atmosphere, fear flourished.

People accused of witchcraft on their way to be hanged.

colonies. The Puritan struggle to keep control was a losing battle. By 1700, some Puritan churches were allowing anyone to attend if they gave money to the church. This was a huge change from a few years before, when the church had power over the community. New England had grown into a diverse society in which religion was only one part of life, and not the most important one.

Small towns appeared all over New England in the 17th and 18th centuries. Along the coast, large ports for fishing and trading developed.

Prosperity and Change

The geography of New England had encouraged an original sense of closeness. The need for small-scale farming in this rocky area meant that New England farmers planted garden vegetables, which they traded with neighbors for other things. This kind of neighborly trade helped knit a town together. But as populations moved farther and farther away from the town centers, the sense of community began to fade.

However, another economy started to grow. New Englanders began to export timber and fish. By the 1660s, New England fishermen and merchants dominated the fishing grounds of the North Atlantic. They traded fish for tobacco from Virginia and sugar from the West Indies. They also traded for manufactured goods from England.

The New England Colonies

N

0   miles   100
0   km   100

Connecticut River

NEW HAMPSHIRE

ATLANTIC OCEAN

Salem
Boston   *Massachusetts Bay*

MASSACHUSETTS

Plymouth

Providence

Hartford   Newport

CONNECTICUT   **RHODE ISLAND**

New Haven

Narragansett Bay

New England Colonies

A wealthy merchant class grew in New England throughout the 1700s. People built luxurious houses filled with European furniture and rode around in fancy carriages. Some had servants and slaves. The number of black people remained small in New England, but New Englanders had no hesitation about owning slaves. In Rhode Island, groups of slaves worked raising livestock. However, slavery was not usually suited to the New England farm, which was a small scale operation. Slaves in the region were concentrated in towns, where they worked as servants and laborers.

Like the Chesapeake Bay region, New England was multicultural, with Indians, black people, and whites (Puritans and non-Puritans). Unlike the Chesapeake, though, the divisions in society were more on economic rather than racial lines. As the 1700s progressed, the rich got richer in New England, but slavery did not take hold.

"We in New England know nothing of poverty and want, we have no idea of the thing, how much better do our poor people live than seven-eighths of the people on this much famed island [Great Britain]."

Connecticut citizen comparing conditions in colonies with those in Britain

Town Meetings

One of the first forms of local government established in the New England colonies was the town meeting. Town meetings still take place in the United States. They are very different from the kinds of meeting in colonial times, but they stem from our colonial past.

Town meetings were a way for people to take part in government that was unheard of in white society at the time. But in the 1600s, the meetings were as yet far from democratic. Indians and black people were of course excluded, as were all women.

Over the centuries, excluded American minorities began to be admitted as voters, and eventually everyone's voice could be heard. Town meetings today are held across the nation, not just in New England. They have a variety of purposes. Few town meetings actually elect officials, but they do provide opportunities for citizens to air their complaints and exchange their points of view. In this way, they influence community decisions. The town meeting is still self-government in operation, and it links people with the officials who serve them.

4

The Middle Colonies

The English colonies of New York, New Jersey, Pennsylvania, and Delaware were known as the Middle Colonies. The king of England had originally granted areas of land in the region to several proprietors. Before the late 1600s, relatively few Europeans settled in this region. For some time the largest colony in the area was made up of a group of Dutch settlements known as New Netherland.

This very early view of New Amsterdam shows a small settlement at the tip of Manhattan Island, in about 1626. The settlement grew slowly until the English took over the colony in 1664. Then New Amsterdam became New York, which in the 1700s expanded to become a city.

The Dutch in North America

In the 1600s, Holland was quite a powerful European country. Although small in territory, it was a strong trading nation with a profitable trade with Asia. In the early 1600s, a group

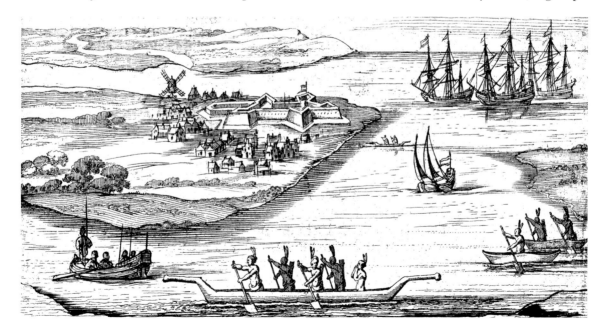

of merchants and shipping companies in Holland formed the Dutch West India Company. The Dutch government granted them exclusive rights to trade in the Western Hemisphere.

In 1624, the West India Company established fur-trading posts on the Hudson River. Two years later, Peter Minuit, the director of the company, "bought" Manhattan Island from a Native American tribe that lived nearby. At the tip of the island was the small Dutch settlement of New Amsterdam. The town was the headquarters of the colony of New Netherland, and the main trading center in the colony.

The West India Company's investment in New Netherland never made a profit. By the 1640s, there were only about 1,500 settlers in New Amsterdam, of which only half were Dutch. The rest were immigrants from Germany, France, and Sweden, among other places. There were also sailors from the West Indies and religious dissenters from other colonies. The area was still home to tribes of Native Americans, too.

The Dutch did not really like governing this mixed bag of inhabitants. They appointed a stern governor, Peter Stuyvesant, who ruled the colony from 1647 to 1664. His policies were disliked by the inhabitants, who wanted more of a voice in governing themselves.

The Dutch had a harsh attitude toward the Indians. Like other Europeans, they traded with Native American groups to their own benefit. They treated those who could help them in a businesslike manner, but others were ruthlessly dealt with. The Dutch provided some tribes with weapons to fight those tribes who opposed Dutch rule.

The Birth of New York

In 1664, England was at war with Holland, and the English decided to carry the conflict to America. A fleet of ships sent by the Duke of York, the brother of the English King Charles II, appeared off Manhattan Island. The English demanded that Stuyvesant surrender and turn the Dutch colony over to their control. Stuyvesant had little choice but to agree.

The English were too powerful to oppose. Few people in the colony would support his resistance anyway. The English took over New Netherland, and the Duke of York was granted an enormous tract of land by his brother, the king. His ambition, like that of other proprietors, was to make money from rent paid by the settlers. New Netherland was renamed New York.

In 1685, the Duke of York succeeded his brother and became King James II. The new king declared New York a royal colony that same year.

The English encouraged settlement in their new colony. Between 1664 and 1700, the population rose

In 1664, the Dutch surrendered the town of New Amsterdam to the English without a fight. Peter Stuyvesant (above, with wooden leg), the governor of New Netherland, was reluctant to give up his unpopular rule.

from about 5,000 to over 20,000. Large grants of lands were awarded to political supporters of the English crown. By the early 1700s, five wealthy families controlled almost two million acres of land along the Hudson River.

They hoped to earn huge sums of money from renting the land. In order to attract settlers, however, the landowners needed to make the move attractive. They often built grain mills and gave the new settlers tools to start their farms. They even offered lower rents to new settlers. Between 1700 and 1760, many more settlers arrived and the owners made a great deal of money.

Rulers from Afar

King Charles II (1630–85) ruled England from 1660 until his death in 1685. It was a period when the English colonies in North America were beginning to grow and prosper, and many of the king's friends profited from grants of land there. His brother, the Duke of York, for whom New York had been named, succeeded Charles II as King James II. But his reign was short-lived. In 1688, a revolution in England caused King James to be overthrown in favor of his daughter Mary and son-in-law William of Orange. Theirs was a joint rule until Mary died in 1694. After William's death in 1702, Mary's sister Anne became queen.

It was during the reign of Queen Anne that England and Scotland joined their governments under the Act of Union in 1707. England had already joined with Wales in 1536. This meant the three countries that made up the island of Great Britain had become one nation. The English colonies in America were officially British colonies from then on.

The Founding of New Jersey

The proprietors of New Jersey did not find their plans so easy to achieve. In 1664, the Duke of York had divided his new grant, giving the area between the Hudson and Delaware Rivers to a new group of proprietors. This grant became the new colony of New Jersey.

New Jersey at that time was home to several thousand Delaware Indians and to a few hundred Dutch and Swedish settlers. By the early 1670s, several thousand New England Puritans had moved to settlements along the New Jersey shore. The newcomers stubbornly refused to pay taxes. In addition, they would not take an oath of loyalty to their new masters. The problems that arose did not make New Jersey an attractive place for other immigrants, and some proprietors became disappointed with their investment. Realizing they would lose money, they sold the region to a group of Quakers. The Quakers divided the territory into the colonies of West Jersey and East Jersey.

New Jersey, like the other Middle Colonies, was settled by farmers. They grew mostly grains, especially wheat. Their flour was sold to other colonies and also exported to Europe.

The new rulers quarreled among themselves, and the governments of both East and West Jersey were troubled. They also were no better at dealing with the Dutch and Puritans than the original proprietors had been. The Quakers soon tired of their troublesome tenants. They gave up their power to the English monarch, and New Jersey became a royal colony in 1702.

Pennsylvania and the Quakers

In 1681, William Penn, a well-known member of the Quakers in England, asked King Charles II for some land in North America. He wanted to found a Quaker colony. The king liked Penn, and he wanted to get rid of the Quakers, who were not liked in England. The king himself originally chose the name "Pensilvania" for the colony, in honor of Penn's father, Admiral Sir William Penn. Penn and his group of followers arrived in the new colony in 1682. He chose a site for the new capital, which he named Philadelphia ("City of Brotherly Love"). He designed streets in neat grids with many gardens.

"The king and country where I live has given unto me a great province therein, but I desire to enjoy it with your love and consent."

William Penn, founder of Pennsylvania

The Quakers

The Quakers were a religious sect founded in England in the 1640s. Their founder, George Fox, was put on trial for his religious beliefs. He warned the judge to "tremble at the word of the Lord." From then on he and his followers were ridiculed as "quakers." Although they called themselves the Religious Society of Friends, the name Quaker stuck.

Quakers believe that an "Inner Light" can inspire every person. Their religious meetings have no leaders or ceremony. People sit in silence until the Inner Light inspires them to stand and speak. To more traditional worshippers, the new religion seemed disrespectful of authority and the church. Quakers refused to tip their hats in public to their social betters. They also refused to use the word "you," which was the usual way a commoner addressed a noble. Instead they used the less formal "thee" or "thou" as a symbol of equality. Equality was important to the Quakers in a time when class divided society and women had few rights.

Many poor people were attracted to the Quakers and by the late 1600s they numbered about 60,000 in England. However, there were many hardships for Quakers: They were fined for not attending Church of England services, their property was often destroyed, and many were whipped or thrown into prison. The opportunity for a new life in the Quaker colony of Pennsylvania appealed to many.

Settlers flocked to the new colony of Pennsylvania. Quakers from England and other countries in Europe came to the new colony, as did many non-Quakers. By the end of the 1680s, more than 8,000 people lived in Pennsylvania. Philadelphia was becoming a thriving city.

Pennsylvania's Government

Pennsylvania as a whole was a flourishing, multicultural colony by the mid-1700s. It had a huge number of German, English, Welsh, and Scottish immigrants. There were also Native American and black populations. Penn believed in religious tolerance, but he was not a pure democrat. He chose to run his colony in an authoritarian manner. This eventually sparked opposition from non-Quaker settlers. In 1701, in response to their demands, Penn granted more power to the local assemblies in the colony.

True to his belief in tolerance, Penn tried to treat the Indians fairly by buying and not simply taking land from

City Life

By the 1700s, the British colonies in North America had a number of fair-sized cities. They included Philadelphia, Boston, New York, and Charleston, South Carolina. Colonists were proud of their cities. European visitors were impressed by Charleston because it had a thriving upper-class social life. But they found other American cities lacking in culture and glamour.

It is true that people in colonial cities still had country ways. In Philadelphia, for example, urban residents still tied up their cows in their backyards. In fact, there were people who made a living by gathering and herding a community's cows in the morning to graze in nearby fields.

Bostonians began to get offended in the 1750s by the poorer inhabitants washing themselves in public. The city passed an ordinance forbidding anyone from removing his or her clothing to wash if they were within ten rods (165 feet, or 50 meters) of a private home. Europeans were not shocked by most aspects of poverty, since their cities were teeming with poor people. Instead, they were amused by the colonists' concern over public nudity.

them. The Delaware Indians got along reasonably well with the new colonists. They saw them as possible allies and protectors from their traditional foe, the Iroquois Confederacy. Later generations of the Penn family did not live up to William Penn's standards. They claimed to abide by his policy, but often misled Indians and sometimes even cheated them.

As a Quaker, Penn disliked governments that had too much power over people. So the colonial government he set up provided for an elected assembly. However, at the same time, it provided for a much stronger governor and governor's council appointed by himself. In addition, the Quakers dominated these early governments. But while Pennsylvania's government was not perfectly democratic, it was at least set up with certain principles of fairness.

In 1683, William Penn signed a peace treaty with the Delaware people in Pennsylvania. The Quakers' more humane attitude to the Indians helped to avoid the conflict that was taking place in other colonies.

Swedish and Finnish people first came to the Delaware River valley in 1638. They built the log cabins that had been their traditional houses in Europe. Today, log cabins are seen as the traditional buildings of the American West. The large rack seen here, also made of logs, is for drying corn.

Like other people who had founded communities based on their ideals, Penn soon discovered that groups of people disagree and quarrel among themselves. As early as the late 1680s, Penn's supporters in the governor's council were arguing with opponents in the assembly to such a degree that the government was almost paralyzed.

Delaware

One of the strongest centers of opposition was on the lower Delaware River, which had become part of Pennsylvania in 1682. It was heavily populated with Dutch and Swedish settlers, who had founded colonies there in the 1630s. In 1704, they were granted their own legislature. This was the beginning of the new colony of Delaware.

Penn's hope for order and peaceful living was also shattered by religious dissent among the Quakers, some of whom wanted a more traditional church. The quarrel shook the colony, and in the end, many Quakers joined the Church of England.

In 1748, Penn's sons, who had inherited proprietorship of the colony, themselves joined the Church of England. The early years of Quaker majority had given way to a mixed society. Settlers from many different countries and religious backgrounds were all intent on pursuing their differing visions of a new life in America.

German and Scotch-Irish Settlers

The Middle Colonies were the destination of thousands of German immigrants. In the 1700s, Germany was not a unified country but a collection of many smaller states.

"Both at Rotterdam and in Amsterdam the people are packed densely, like herrings so to say, in the large sea vessels. One person receives a place of scarcely 2 feet width and 6 feet length in the bedstead."

German immigrant Gottlieb Mittelberger, describing crowded immigrant ships

Mary Jemison (1743–1833)

Mary Jemison was a colonist who lived in western Pennsylvania. She was born on board a ship carrying her parents from Ireland to America. In 1758, during the French and Indian War, Mary was captured by the French and taken to Fort Duquesne, Pennsylvania. She was given to two Seneca Indian women who adopted her. Jemison came to love the Seneca. They treated her kindly and accepted her as one of their own.

Mary lived the rest of her life among the Indians. She married twice, to a Delaware and a Seneca, and chose to live as an adopted Seneca. Known as the "White Woman of the Genesee," she lived on land given to her by the Seneca in the 1790s. In 1824, when she was in her 80s, she was interviewed by James E. Seaver about her life with the Indians. The interview was published in a book called *A Narrative of the Life of Mary Jemison; Deh-He-Wa-Mis*.

The book is an important account of life among New York Indians. At the time, Indians were regarded as "savages," and their cultural differences were considered threatening by white people. Jemison's description of their society was a rare view of Native Americans as human beings, not just heathens in need of conversion.

During Queen Anne's War (1702-1713), French forces invaded the German region of Palatinate, just over the border from France. It was from this area especially that Germans fled to the American colonies. By 1770, more than 100,000 had arrived, and most settled in Pennsylvania. The majority were farmers and laborers, attracted by the availability of land in the colony.

Another group of immigrants was referred to as the "Scotch-Irish," which could be misleading. Some were indeed Scottish people who had settled in northern Ireland at an earlier time. Others were just pure Irish, or from Scotland or northern England. To American colonists, however, they all seemed alike and therefore were grouped under one name.

The Amish sect began in 1693 when a group of Mennonites broke away from their main church and adopted a stricter way of life. Today, the Amish people in Pennsylvania still reject modern technology. Their vehicles and farm machinery are pulled by horses. They make many things themselves, keeping alive traditional American crafts such as quilt-making.

Both the German and Scotch-Irish immigrants were Protestants of one kind or another. Most Germans were Lutherans, while others belonged to a variety of dissenter sects like the Moravians, the Dunkers, the Mennonites, and the Amish. The Scotch-Irish were almost all Presbyterians. German and Scotch-Irish people preferred to live in communities with their fellow countrymen. To some of the early colonists, they seemed to be "taking over" the colony from the English founders.

54

Panic grew among the white residents of New York City when a series of fires took place in 1741. Many people suspected black slaves of starting a rebellion. Several slaves were hanged or burned alive, even though there was no real evidence that they were guilty.

Slavery in the Middle Colonies

The African American population of the Middle Colonies in 1770 was about 30,000. Almost all were slaves, and most lived in New York City. There were only about 3,000 black people in Philadelphia. The Dutch in New Netherland had encouraged the importation of slaves, but the Quakers were

"A new Negro will require more discipline than a young spaniel."

Comment by a colonist in 1740 about slaves

mostly against the practice. This explained the difference in the slave populations of the two colonies.

Most slaves in the Middle Colonies were servants or laborers, as in New England. Slaves in the Middle Colonies were not much better off than those in the Chesapeake or Southern Colonies. Whites regarded blacks as inferior and treated them as such. Slaves had no rights or legal protection. They were governed by their masters, not by the law. Runaway slaves or those who were not cooperative enough were often whipped with great brutality.

Sometimes worse things happened. In New York City in 1741, 13 slaves were burned at the stake and another 18 hanged because authorities suspected a conspiracy to take over the city. There was, it turned out, no conspiracy, but the slaves were still killed, along with four white people.

Expanding Outward

New immigrants arrived throughout the 1700s, with greater numbers coming at times when economic conditions were bad in Europe. The vast majority arrived under a form of indentured servitude. A ship's captain would transport them to America, where the immigrants' passage would be paid by friends or relatives already in the colonies. Those not lucky enough to have someone waiting to pay their debt would sell themselves as servants.

Their hope was that they would eventually work off their debt and acquire freedom and a small farm. This proved difficult, and in many cases impossible. But immigrants during these years were prepared to take the risk rather than remain in Europe, where poverty was widespread and the threat of war was always present.

As more and more immigrants arrived, settlers in the Middle Colonies moved farther and farther westward. By the middle of the century, settlers were already on the eastern slopes of the Appalachian Mountains. Other communities were being established in the Shenandoah Valley in Virginia, and sometimes as far south as the Carolinas.

Food in the Colonies

Many of the foods we find on our table today were available to the colonists of North America. There were all kinds of meat: beef, chicken, turkey, and rabbit were plentiful. Fish was in good supply. People could grow vegetables, such as potatoes, turnips, peas, and beans. Corn, to which the Indians had introduced the first white settlers, soon became a staple food. Fruit such as apples, peaches, and cranberries were also grown in the colonies.

This choice meant that the diet of most settlers was much better than that of poor people in Europe. But by today's standards, their diet would not be considered healthy. In the 1700s, colonists had little understanding about the benefits of eating vegetables and fruit. Instead they actually believed that raw vegetables were unhealthy. As a result, their diets were heavy in salted and smoked meats. In the days before refrigeration, salting and smoking were used to prevent meat from rotting. Those vegetables that were eaten were usually overcooked or pickled.

These eating habits tended to be the same for the rich as well as the poor. The main difference was that the rich could afford better-quality meat.

One of the worst aspects of the colonial diet was the amount of alcohol drunk. Alcoholic beverages, especially ale and beer, were drunk at breakfast time and throughout the day. Doctors even prescribed beer for nursing mothers and wine to cure the disease of tuberculosis. Any pain was also treated with some form of alcoholic beverage. It was a long time before people learned the nutritional importance of fruits and vegetables, and the bad effects of too much animal fat and alcohol.

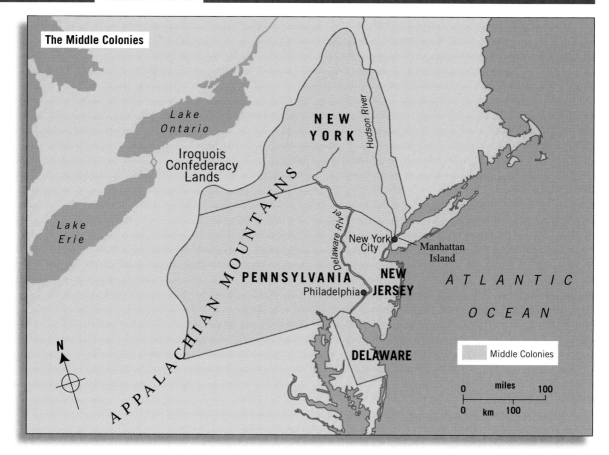

The Middle Colonies

Lake Ontario

NEW YORK

Hudson River

Iroquois Confederacy Lands

Lake Erie

APPALACHIAN MOUNTAINS

Delaware River

PENNSYLVANIA

Philadelphia

NEW JERSEY

New York City

Manhattan Island

A T L A N T I C

O C E A N

N

DELAWARE

Middle Colonies

miles
0   100

0   km   100

By the 1700s, the Middle Colonies had become a thriving agricultural area. Wheat and flour became the main sources of wealth, and the colonial years were a time of prosperity for the farmers.

Not many settlers ventured directly north of Pennsylvania, however. This area was dominated by the powerful Iroquois Confederacy. These Indians were strong enough to defend their territory from the advance of colonists. Few settlers risked moving into western or northern New York when they could enjoy the peaceful countryside of Pennsylvania.

Economic Growth

The Middle Colonies, especially Pennsylvania, developed into a region of wheat and flour production. In the 1700s, there was great demand for wheat in the colonies, the West Indies, and Europe.

Farmers could sell their wheat for cash in North America, and this money allowed them to buy tools, livestock, consumer products, and more land. Their wheat was traded extensively in European countries, which tied the colonies' economy to that of Europe.

From a region that was sparsely settled in the early 1600s, the Middle Colonies emerged as an economic powerhouse by the mid-1700s. Like New England and the Chesapeake, the area was a mixture of Indians, Africans, English, German, Scotch-Irish, and others. The religious goals that the early founders had hoped for gave way to economic purposes.

African Burial Ground

Today the southern tip of Manhattan Island in New York City is packed with government and commercial buildings. It bustles with traffic and people. Despite its modern appearance, this is one of the oldest parts of New York. It is the site of some of the earliest settlements in Dutch colonial times.

In the early 1990s, construction workers were digging deep into the earth to make foundations for a new courthouse, just two blocks from City Hall. As they dug, the workers made an extraordinary discovery. About 16 feet (4.5 m) below the surface of the street, they uncovered the remnants of a burial ground from colonial times.

What the workers had found was part of a cemetery for black people who had lived in New York in the late 1700s. Like almost everything else for black people at that time, their cemeteries were separate from those for white people. About 400 people, almost half of them children, were buried there. In addition to bones, archaeologists have found buttons, rings, glass beads, and pins.

The fact that so many children were buried in the graves reveals the high death rate among African children in colonial times. Scientists can also find out more about what people ate in those days by examining the teeth of skeletons. The African Burial Ground tells us much about the lives of black people more than 200 years ago.

5

The Southern Colonies

T he southern region of the British colonies was made up
of North Carolina, South Carolina, and Georgia. They
are sometimes known as the Lower South, while the
Chesapeake Colonies of Virginia and Maryland are referred
to as the Upper South. The Upper and Lower South shared
many social and cultural characteristics, despite their
individual differences.

The Founding of the Carolinas

The first permanent white settlements in North Carolina
were founded near Albemarle Sound, just south of Virginia,
in 1653. These settlers came from Virginia and moved into
what had recently become "Carolina." This was a huge land
grant made by the English king to Sir Robert Heath. To
encourage more settlement, the area was re-granted to eight
new proprietors in 1663. One of these was Sir William
Berkeley, then governor of Virginia.

The population of the region remained small, with only
some 4,000 residents by 1700. Most of the settlers stayed in
the Albemarle Sound area, where they raised tobacco, corn,
and livestock. Some farms had indentured servants as well
as a small number of black and Indian slaves.

North Carolina

In 1711, North Carolina became a separate colony. Soon
afterward, a destructive war broke out with the native
Tuscarora people. The Indians were defeated and driven
north, where they joined the Iroquois Confederacy. Other

Much of the Carolinas was heavily forested and hard to reach. Remote homesteads such as this one were threatened in the Tuscarora War of 1711-12, when the Indian population attacked white settlers who had moved onto their lands.

Indian tribes were gradually pushed back toward the Appalachian Mountains as Germans and Scotch-Irish settlers from Pennsylvania began moving onto their lands.

North Carolina was rough territory. Its thick forests made overland travel almost impossible, and large boats found it difficult to navigate the waterways around the many islands off the coast. The white settlers in this isolated area were hardy souls, not afraid to disagree with the more "cultured" Virginians. Other Southerners thought of North Carolinians as "quarrelsome and lazy" (in the words of William Byrd, a rich Virginian planter).

The North Carolinian spirit of independence showed itself in the late 1760s, when farmers in the western part of the colony rebelled against their government. They protested at their high taxes and lack of protection against hostile Indians. They set up courts and government bodies to

Charleston, South Carolina, is full of historic buildings. The Old Exchange Building, built in colonial times, became City Hall in 1873.

"Many people of the genteeler sort keep handsome Four Wheel'd Carriages, horses, Coachmen, and all imported from England."

English traveler on Charleston, South Carolina

regulate their own affairs. This became known as the "Regulator Movement." The movement was suppressed after a few years. In a battle with government forces in 1771, the Regulators were defeated. Some of their leaders were found guilty of treason and executed.

South Carolina

During the 1500s, both the Spanish and the French tried to found settlements in what is now South Carolina, but they were finally pushed out by the English in 1629. After the change of proprietorship in 1663, the southern part of the Carolinas developed separately from the northern part.

In 1670, an English settlement was built at Albemarle Point. (This is not the same as Albemarle Sound in North Carolina.) In 1680, the settlement moved to the other side of the Ashley River and was renamed Charles Town. Charles Town became the center of wealth and culture in the colony. It is now the city of Charleston.

The white settlers began to set up plantations that were run with the labor of black and Indian slaves. Crops included tobacco, corn, and some cotton. Rice was introduced in the marshy coastal areas, where it grew well. Soon it became the most profitable crop grown in the colony. Another good moneymaker for the settlers was their trade in deerskin with the Creek Indians.

In 1719, South Carolinians set up their own government, and in 1721 South Carolina became a royal colony. White immigration into the colony increased in the 1730s. Germans, Scotch-Irish, and other migrants from Virginia and Pennsylvania settled the lower and middle parts of the colony. The new settlers, most of whom were small farmers, formed a different society from that of the wealthy planters along the coast. Because of this, regional rivalries soon developed in South Carolina.

The Georgia Buffer Zone

To the south of the colony was a power that South Carolinians considered a menace: Spanish Florida. The British government wanted to create a buffer zone. This was an area that would separate the two regions, and so protect South Carolina from attacks by Spanish forces. The guiding force in the creation of a colony in this area was James Oglethorpe, an English politician who was committed to helping the poor and imprisoned. In 1733, Oglethorpe and 19 others became the trustees of a 21-year charter to found Georgia, hoping it could be a place to send imprisoned debtors from Britain, who would then guard against attacks by the Spanish.

Oglethorpe and a party of more than 100 men set out to create the new colony. In 1733, they founded the town of Savannah and established relations with the Yamacraw Creek Indians. Turning their attention to the south, the new settlers began building fortifications against the Spanish in Florida.

Oglethorpe encouraged settlers from the European continent as well as from Britain. In its early years, the colony was multinational, with settlers arriving from Germany, Italy, Switzerland, and France. However, settlers from the other American colonies were banned from

In the 1730s and 1740s, many immigrants flooded into Georgia. Among them were Scottish people who built the settlement of New Inverness. They were visited in 1736 by the governor of Georgia, James Oglethorpe, seen here in traditional Scottish costume.

James Oglethorpe (1696-1785)

James Oglethorpe served as a Member of Parliament in the British House of Commons for more than 30 years. During his government service, Oglethorpe became interested in the plight of debtors. The need for a buffer colony between South Carolina and Florida coincided nicely with Oglethorpe's suggestion for a haven to which debtors could migrate.

After founding the colony of Georgia, Oglethorpe played another role there before returning to England. He led a number of military raids into Florida against the Spanish. In June 1742, he defeated a Spanish force at the battle of Bloody Marsh. This victory assured the survival of the colony against Spanish attacks. A year later, Oglethorpe tried unsuccessfully to capture the city of St. Augustine in Spanish Florida. By now, many of the colonists were sick of Oglethorpe, his ideals, and his rigid management. He was recalled to England and never returned to Georgia.

"Ordinary Women take care of Cows, Hogs, and other small Cattle, make butter and Cheese, spin Cotton and Flax, help to sow and reap Corn, wind Silk, gather Fruit, and look after the House."

Traveler describing women's work in the South, 1704

moving into Georgia. Oglethorpe was opposed to slavery and had Parliament outlaw it in the colony. He also tried to keep landholdings small in order to encourage small farmers to settle there.

The first immigrants in Georgia fell into two groups. Debtors or other "charity settlers" were financed by the colony's trustees. Other settlers paid their own way and received the best land grants. Oglethorpe and the trustees hoped the colony would produce silk, which could be sold in England. To this end, early settlers were required to plant mulberry trees for the breeding of silkworms which feed on the leaves. However, the colony was never able to cultivate enough silkworms to make silk production profitable.

Oglethorpe banned alcohol from the new colony. This law was unpopular, and so was the slavery ban and the limit on the size of landholdings. Colonists were fond of their rum and not willing to give it up. They also wanted the right to expand their property and to have slaves work their land. Settlement stayed low while Oglethorpe's policies were in force.

The Southern Colonies

The Southern Colonies, like the Chesapeake Colonies, developed into an area of plantations. Their main crops were rice and indigo, a plant grown to make blue dye. North Carolina was also the main region in the South for raising livestock.

In 1750, the trustees lifted the ban on slavery and allowed larger landholdings. The ban on alcohol was also lifted, and in the next 20 years the population boomed. In 1750, there were already more than 1,000 illegal slaves in Georgia. By 1770, slaves made up 45 percent of the population, which then stood at 23,000.

One original purpose of the plan did succeed. Georgia indeed proved to be a buffer zone against Spanish plans for settling north of Florida. The Georgia colony completed the British occupation of the Atlantic coast. In all the colonies, the population continued to grow and take over more land, even though settlers did not immediately push west of the Appalachians. And as the white population in British North America grew, so did the population of slaves.

Early American Slave Trade

Africans first arrived in the Chesapeake region in 1619 as laborers. Slavery as a legal institution had not yet evolved in the colonies. That came later, as the indentured servant system broke down. Over time, planters in the South became more and more dependent on slave labor for growing tobacco and rice.

The first Africans were brought to the Americas by the Spanish. During the 1700s, the slave trade was conducted by many other European nations, including the English, French, Portuguese, and Dutch. Hundreds of thousands of people were taken from their homelands in Africa. They may have been taken captive in African wars and then sold to Europeans. Others were kidnapped outright. They were crammed in chains into the holds of sailing ships, and shipped thousands of miles to the West Indies, South America, or the North American colonies. This brutal voyage across the Atlantic is known as the "Middle Passage."

Millions of Africans were brought across the Atlantic Ocean between 1520 and 1810, and not just to North America. More than 4 million were transported to South America, and over 3 million to the West Indies.

The Middle Passage

Some slavers packed their slaves loosely into the ship, on the theory that more of them would survive and be in better condition for sale once they reached America. Others filled

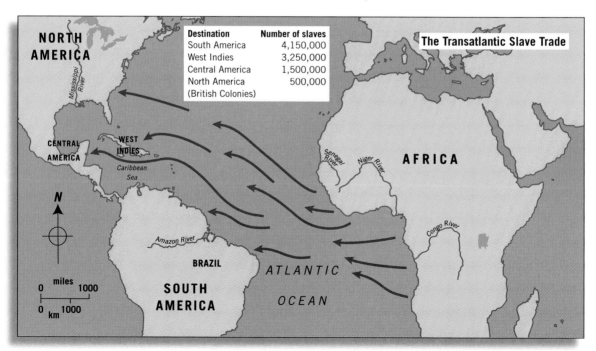

Destination	Number of slaves
South America	4,150,000
West Indies	3,250,000
Central America	1,500,000
North America (British Colonies)	500,000

The Transatlantic Slave Trade

The Middle Passage was the journey made by captured slaves from Africa to North or South America. In conditions of unbelievable horror, millions of Africans were transported from their homeland to a life of captivity, cruelty, and unpaid labor.

their ship holds with as many slaves as possible, knowing that the crowded conditions would lead to many deaths. They believed that they would still have more survivors at the end of the voyage, and then there would be more profits from sales.

For the slaver, the most dangerous time of the trip was when the vessel was anchored off the coast of West Africa. This is where they loaded slaves for the voyage west. Slaves had to be captured and transported to the coast, and filling a ship with hundreds of slaves took several weeks. During this time, slaves sometimes mutinied and tried to escape back to shore. Africans did not submit tamely to being chained and carted across the Atlantic. Attacks were also made against the anchored slave ships from ashore, and by pirates who roamed the coast of Africa.

"We choose Negroes from several parts of the country, of different languages; so that they cannot act jointly, when they are not in a capacity of consulting one another, and this they cannot do insofar as they understand not one another".

Captain of slave ship explaining why they mixed slaves from different parts of Africa

Olaudah Equiano (c.1745–?)

Firsthand accounts by those captured in Africa and brought to the Americas as slaves are almost nonexistent. One major exception is the writings of Olaudah Equiano, who was born in what is now Nigeria. He was kidnapped at the age of 11 along with his sister, and dragged into slavery.

After several months in captivity in Africa, he was placed on a slave ship bound for Barbados in the West Indies. He eventually ended up in Philadelphia, where he was bought by a Quaker merchant. Equiano was permitted to buy his freedom from his Quaker owner. In his mid-20s, he moved to England. There he adopted an English way of life and became something of a celebrity. There is even a painting of him in the clothes of an 18th-century English gentleman, complete with wig. But Equiano never forgot his African roots.

In 1789, Equiano published a book under the name Gustavus Vasa, entitled *The Interesting Narrative of the Life of Olaudah Equiano or Gustavus Vasa, Written by Himself.* The narrative was a chilling and heartrending tale of his captivity and separation from his sister. It told of the dreadful Middle Passage voyage across the Atlantic to the West Indies, and his early years as a slave in North America. His relentless description of the slave trade was an eloquent plea for an end to slavery.

Once at sea, the opportunity for mutiny and escape was gone. The slaves were now at the mercy of the ship's captain. If the weather was clear, the slaves were brought on deck during the day. The men were chained at both sides of the ship, while the women and small children were allowed to wander. In the morning they were fed their first meal on deck. This would be either boiled rice, cornmeal, or stewed yams, and a cup of water.

Next came a practice called "dancing the slaves." Those in chains were required to move around as best they could, in the belief that this would guard against suicidal thoughts and illnesses. For the slaves the movement was very painful because of their shackled legs and arms.

Slaves on deck had to be watched to prevent them from committing suicide by jumping overboard. Some Africans believed that if they died their spirits would return to their homelands. In order to discourage slaves from taking their own lives, the captain of one slave ship cut the head off an African who had committed suicide and showed it to the other slaves. If anyone committed suicide, he said, he would make sure that his or her spirit went home without its head!

The slave holds below deck were cleaned during the day when the slaves were up on deck. Some captains were more strict than others about cleaning the slave holds because they feared that illness could wipe out their entire cargo. This was a task no one wanted to do. The conditions below deck, with so many people crowded together, were extremely dirty and unhealthy. Despite the cleaning, living conditions were extremely horrible. Slaves were often packed so tightly together that they could only lie on their sides when they were sleeping.

In the afternoon, the slaves were given their second meal. It sometimes consisted of a kind of bean that they were not familiar with and found difficult to eat. After the meal, the slaves were put below deck and locked in for the night. Crew members would often hear them weeping and crying in anguish as they thought about their homeland and the terrible conditions they were now in.

"The first object which saluted my eyes when I arrived on the coast was the sea, and a slaveship, which was then riding at anchor, and waiting for its cargo. These filled me with astonishment, which was soon converted into terror, which I am yet at a loss to describe. . . . The stench of the hold while we were on the coast, was so intolerably loathsome, that it was dangerous to remain there for any time. . . . The shrieks of the women and the groans of the dying, rendered the whole scene a horror almost inconceivable."

Olaudah Equiano describing his experience on a slave ship

During rain and storms, the slaves were kept below all day. The air became hot and difficult to breathe. During these times, many slaves became sick and died. Some went insane and were beaten to death by the crew.

On the last day or two of the voyage, the slaves were usually fed more and allowed to drink all the water they wanted. The captains wanted the slaves to appear as healthy as possible for the sale that was to take place as soon as they went ashore. Slaves who were still ill from the trip could also be fattened up in a West Indian slave pen before being put up for auction.

The slave sale varied from place to place. In the West Indies, a middleman called a factor would often buy a whole group of slaves and then sell them individually to buyers.

A poster advertising a slave auction.

Slaves who were ill or old were usually auctioned off for small amounts. Healthy slaves were sold at what became known as a "scramble." The prices were agreed upon beforehand and the purchasers then scrambled for their pick of the slaves.

Slave Resistance

The tobacco planters of the Chesapeake and the rice planters of South Carolina expected their slaves to work long, punishing days. When the Africans resisted, the threat of physical punishment was ever present. Slave owners discussed at length the wisdom and necessity of disciplining their slaves. The most common form of punishment was whipping.

Resistance continued over the years, and at times rebellion broke out. In 1739, a slave rebellion occurred in Stono, South Carolina. Some 20 slaves attacked a country store and killed its owners, and then made off with guns and ammunition. Their goal, apparently, was to escape to Spanish Florida. On the way, the slaves attacked some plantations and killed more than 20 white people. A group of determined whites pursued the rebels and eventually caught up with them. Many were killed and their heads were displayed on posts along the road as a warning to other slaves.

Auctions were very profitable for slave traders. African people were sold like animals to white colonists. Buyers looked for healthy, strong slaves who would be able to work hard.

Stono showed how little chance the slaves had for rebelling against slavery. South Carolina made stricter laws because of the Stono uprising. Slaves understood that survival would have to be within the limits of slavery. But they could, and did, resist their masters in many clever ways. At times, they would take part in work slowdowns, especially when being supervised in large numbers. They also sabotaged equipment, and occasionally even poisoned their masters using skills learned in Africa.

Slave Life in the 1700s

Slaves were held in captivity, but they were not just quiet victims. Through it all, they also tried to create families. Most of them had been torn apart from their families of birth. Wives, husbands, and children from their African families were lost forever. In America, they made new families. They met other Africans, and new relationships were formed. Much remains unknown about the networks that slaves formed in the 1700s. However, historians do know that family relationships were very important. Slave parents often gave a child the name of an African family member, a sure sign that they honored their preslavery relationships.

Many traditional American crafts actually came from other continents. Sweet grass baskets are associated with the American south, but they were introduced by African slaves.

Slaves contributed to the growth of colonies by applying many of their African skills and techniques. In South Carolina, for example, the climate was similar to many parts of West Africa. African-style fishing nets were in widespread use, as were African baskets, and canoes. Some Africans still practiced their old religions, or brought parts of their rituals to their new lives. African skills, names, traditions, and even remnants of language were passed down in various forms from one generation to another. Although they were held in captivity, Africans in America created their own way of life.

Some sections of the South, South Carolina for example, developed black majorities. Southern culture became more and more shaped by slavery. It was of central importance to the economy, and it affected the thinking and actions of white people in many ways. A huge division based on race grew up in Southern society.

Gullah

In the South, especially in the Sea Islands off the coast of South Carolina and Georgia, a distinctive language developed among the slaves. Called "Gullah," it was a mix of 17th- and 18th-century English and a number of West African tongues. These included the languages of Hausa, Ibo, and Yoruba.

Gullah can still be heard among some longtime residents of the Sea Islands. Some African words in Gullah have entered the English language, including *goober* (peanut) and *gumbo* (okra). Slave masters often thought they were mixing members of African tribes who spoke different languages. But there was a considerable overlap in culture and language among groups from West Africa. The development of a distinctive language among the many slaves in the islands was one way they formed bonds and a sense of community.

"We are deprived of every thing that hath a tendency to make life more tolerable, the endearing ties of husband and wife we are strangers to, for we are no longer man and wife than our masters or mistresses thinks proper married or unmarried. Our children are taken from us by force and sent many miles from us where we seldom ever see them again."

Petition for freedom by slaves, mid-1700s

The French and Indian War

This map was made in 1755 by the Society of Anti-Gallicans. (Anti-Gallicans were people who were against the French.) The map shows the areas that the British believed were threatened by the French. At the side it shows plans of some French forts.

During the 1700s, Britain was often at war with France. Several times their conflicts spilled over into the Americas. In the 1750s, rivalry between the French and British increased into the French and Indian War.

The French were established in New Orleans and at isolated forts along the Mississippi River. They also controlled what is now Canada. The British, of course, were settled in New England and southward along the Atlantic coast. The colonists of New England were the closest to the French settlements in Quebec and Montreal, as well as to the lands of Native Americans who were allied with the French.

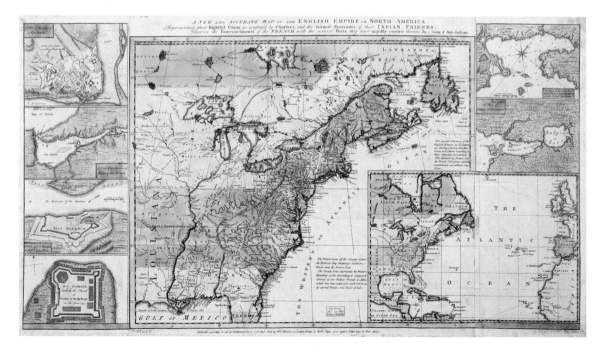

In the 1750s, the French began moving into Indian lands in western New York, Pennsylvania, and into the Ohio River valley. They hoped to expand their trade connections, including those with Indian nations. And they wanted to stop the British expanding westward.

Clashes in the West

British colonists living in Virginia also wanted to move into some of these areas. Some Virginians even believed that their colony's territory extended as far west as the Mississippi River. To advance these claims, a group of Virginians formed the Ohio Company. In 1749, the company obtained from the British king a large grant of land in what is now western Pennsylvania.

In December 1753, George Washington delivered a letter to the commander of the French forces at Lake Erie. In the letter, the British claimed the entire Ohio River valley.

To the north, on Lake Erie, was a large French military force. In 1753, the governor of Virginia decided to send a messenger to warn the French that they were trespassing on Virginian land when they entered the Ohio River valley. That messenger was 21-year-old George Washington, whose older brothers were shareholders in the Ohio Company. While on his mission, Washington made careful notes about the size of the French forces. Back in Virginia, he reported this information to the governor, and told him that force would be needed to remove the French from the region.

In 1754, the Ohio Company began building a fort near the modern-day city of Pittsburgh. This was never finished, as French forces took over the fort and renamed it Fort Duquesne. In the spring of 1754, the governor of Virginia ordered Washington to raise troops and seek out the French.

The Young George Washington (1732–99)

George Washington, whose face we see every day on a dollar bill, was born on February 22, 1732, in Westmoreland County, Virginia. His father was Augustine Washington and his mother Mary Ball Washington. They were wealthy landowners.

George Washington began to take on responsibilities at an early age. At the age of 17, he was appointed surveyor of the newly created Culpepper County. Through his older half-brother, Lawrence Washington, he became interested in the Ohio Company, which was formed to develop western lands. When Lawrence died in 1752, George Washington was only 20, but he took over many of Lawrence's responsibilities. At about the same time, he was given the job of training militia in his district.

Washington came to public notice with his military involvement in the French and Indian War, during which he rose to command the Virginia militia. He seemed destined to play a major role in the affairs of his country. Washington went on to become commander in chief of the Continental Army in the American Revolution, and then the first president of the United States.

Washington's authority and presence showed clearly in his early years. He stood 6 feet, 3 inches tall, which in those days was unusually large. Besides a striking physical appearance, he had a great talent to lead. People responded to him and believed he was special. Something else made Washington seem extraordinary. Despite the numerous battles he fought, and many close calls (including having horses shot out from under him), he never once suffered a scratch in combat.

Washington gathered about 150 men and headed for the Ohio River valley. He was joined by Native Americans in the area. Even with the aid of the Indians, the Virginians were hopelessly outnumbered in battle with the French and their Indian allies. Washington himself was captured by the French. He was soon released, with instructions to tell the Virginians that the French had no intention of giving up the west.

Organizing for War

The British were not about to give in to the French. The government in London decided to organize the colonies to defend themselves. They ordered the Virginia authorities to send representatives to Albany, New York, and meet with delegates from other colonies to plan their strategy.

The Albany Congress, which met in June 1754, consisted of 24 delegates from seven colonies. (Not all the colonies were concerned about the French presence in the Ohio River valley.) Among those present was Benjamin Franklin from Pennsylvania, a man who would play a major role in American history.

The Albany Congress discussed the French alliances with Indian tribes. They hoped to persuade some member tribes of the Iroquois Confederacy to ally with the British. Representatives of the Iroquois attended the conference, including delegates of the Seneca, Mohawk, and Tuscarora tribes. They left without ever pledging to fight the French. Instead, they adopted a wait-and-see attitude, wanting to commit themselves to the side that was sure of victory. In 1754, that side did not appear to be the British.

The Albany Congress called for a colonial administration to plan the defense of the colonies. The British and the colonies never acted on this suggestion, but an important seed had been sown. Some of the colonies had met to discuss their common future.

The Battle for America

By 1755, the British had decided to attack French forces in several different locations. They hoped the attacks would drive the French out of the west and back into Canada. The first encounter was at Fort Duquesne. A force under General Edward

The British General Braddock was defeated by the French and their Native American allies in 1755. The Native Americans were armed with European weapons but also with a knowledge of their country. This helped them to take Braddock's forces by surprise.

Braddock's Campaign

One of the reasons General Edward Braddock was sent to the colonies to fight the French was because of his vast knowledge of military tactics. He had gained this experience on the battlefields of Europe.

For his attack on Fort Duquesne, Braddock left Virginia with a force of 700 colonial militiamen and 1,400 regular British troops. The march went slowly as Braddock's force made its way through dense forests. Braddock feared that the French would reinforce Duquesne before he arrived. So he took two-thirds of his men and pushed ahead, leaving wagons and the rest of the men behind. The militiamen tried to tell Braddock about Indian-style fighting, but he dismissed their warnings because he didn't consider them to be professional soldiers. As they crossed the Monongahela River, they were ambushed by a force of Frenchmen and Indians. Safely hidden in trees and rocks, the French and Native Americans opened fire on the British troops, who fled in terror.

Hundreds of men were killed or wounded. Braddock himself had four horses shot out from under him, and then he too was shot. He died four days later.

Braddock's unfortunate experience showed that much was still to be learned about how to fight in the wilderness, especially against an enemy who called it home. It was also an example of the divide between the colonists and the British regulars. Disagreements marked their relations throughout the war and helped set the stage for the conflicts that led to the American Revolution.

Braddock was supposed to surprise the French and seize the fort. But before they even arrived at Fort Duquesne they were ambushed by a French force. More than 900 men were killed or wounded, and the survivors returned to Virginia. George Washington, who was a member of Braddock's army, was not hurt. He was rewarded for his bravery in battle by being made the head of all the Virginia forces.

Braddock's defeat began a period of two years during which the British made no advances. The French remained at their forts in the west and were joined by a number of Indian tribes. The Indians had allied themselves with what appeared to be the winning side.

In 1757, the British decided to commit more forces in an effort to win the French and Indian War. William Pitt, the British secretary of state, sent a large and better-equipped force to the colonies. He was also able to persuade some of the colonies to spend more money on their defense, promising to pay them back later for all expenditures.

Under Pitt's guidance, the tide turned in 1758. British forces led by General Jeffrey Amherst captured Fort Louisbourg on Cape Breton Island in Canada. They also attempted to take Fort Duquesne again, and this time they succeeded. The French were driven out and the fort was renamed Fort Pitt, in honor of the British minister. (Fort Pitt eventually became Pittsburgh.) In 1759, Fort Niagara was taken by General William Johnson. His army was made up of British and colonial troops assisted by more than a thousand Iroquois. Next to fall was Fort Ticonderoga on Lake Champlain, which surrendered to Amherst.

Defeat of the French

The collapse of French positions at Niagara and Ticonderoga meant that the way was now clear for the British to advance north and attack Montreal and Quebec. The decisive battle of the war was fought at Quebec in 1759. The fortress city

General Washington (center) watches as the British flag is raised over Fort Duquesne, renamed Fort Pitt by the British. The capture of Fort Duquesne in 1758 was an important victory for the British. It was from here that the French had controlled trade in the upper Ohio River valley.

The commanders of both forces were killed in the British attack on the French at Quebec in 1759. The final battle was brief, but the British had laid siege to the capital of New France for more than two months.

was perched on a rocky cliff and defended by the French general Marquis de Montcalm. The British, under General James Wolfe, bombarded the city and surrounding area with fierce cannon fire.

After weeks of scorching fire that set the city aflame, Wolfe ordered his men to scale the cliffs in the dead of night. Before the French realized it, a sizable British force had climbed up the cliffs and assembled on a flat area called the Plains of Abraham. The French responded too late to drive out the British. They were quickly defeated in a battle that saw both Montcalm and Wolfe killed.

In 1760, the French army in Montreal surrendered. The war in North America had come to an end. Battles went on for two more years in the Caribbean. During 1762, several Caribbean islands, starting with the French base Martinique, fell under British control.

The Treaty of Paris
In 1763, the Treaty of Paris officially ended the French and Indian War. France had already given its lands west of the Mississippi River to Spain the year before. Under the treaty, France also gave up its claims to Canada and Acadia (Nova Scotia). All these areas came under British control. Florida was passed from Spain to Britain. Under the Treaty of Paris,

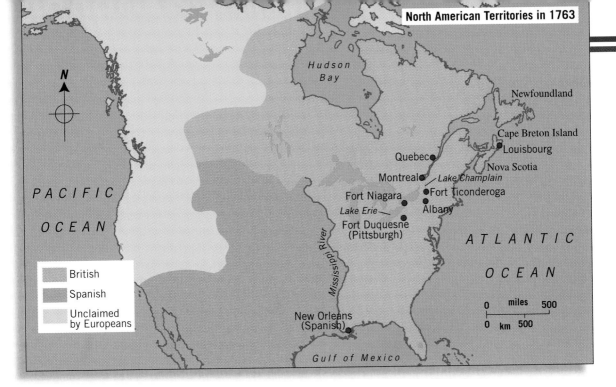

Hudson Bay

Newfoundland

Cape Breton Island
Louisbourg
Quebec
Nova Scotia
Montreal — Lake Champlain
Fort Niagara — Fort Ticonderoga
Lake Erie — Albany
Fort Duquesne
(Pittsburgh)

PACIFIC

OCEAN

ATLANTIC

OCEAN

Mississippi River

British
Spanish
Unclaimed by Europeans

New Orleans
(Spanish)

miles 500
0 km 500

Gulf of Mexico

the British gained all the French territory east of the Mississippi, except the city of New Orleans.

The treaty completely ignored the Indians, however. Their lands were assigned to British control on the map, but no one had consulted the Indians. The treaty had removed the French from North America, but this was not necessarily a good thing for the Native Americans.

British-Colonial Relations

The French and Indian War marked the onset of ill-feeling between the colonists and their British governors. It seemed to the British that the colonists had fought the war very unwillingly. They had been slow to provide troops and money until Pitt had promised to repay them. In addition, many colonists had continued to engage in smuggling with French traders, both in Canada and the Caribbean. This fact greatly annoyed the British who had spent a fortune fighting the war. They felt the colonists should pay some of the costs.

The colonists felt that they had already paid in blood. They did not want to be taxed to pay for the war. This was particularly true in New England, where a huge number of

British territories in North America were vastly expanded after the Treaty of Paris in 1763. The British had dealt with the threat from the French. But their control of the colonies was soon to be challenged from within.

81

Benjamin Franklin (1706–90)

Benjamin Franklin was one of the outstanding figures of American history. He was an immortal product of colonial America and a founder of the United States. Franklin was also a writer, scientist, and printer.

Franklin was born in Boston, the son of a candle and soap maker. He left school at the age of ten to help his father. He then learned the printing trade by working for his half-brother James. He left Boston for Philadelphia in 1723, where he bought a publication called *The Pennsylvania Gazette*. The *Gazette* became very successful under his ownership.

Franklin had the ability to write clever phrases, and in 1732 he began publishing them in a yearly book called *Poor Richard's Almanac*. Poor Richard praised common sense and honesty, and many of the sayings became well-known American proverbs. Franklin was a founder of the American Philosophical Society, and of an academy that became the University of Pennsylvania.

As Franklin grew older, he became increasingly interested in scientific experiments. He was so successful that he is now recognized as an important inventor. He was interested especially in electricity, and his daring experiment of flying a kite in a thunderstorm proved the presence of electricity in lightning. He also invented the lightning rod, bifocal eyeglasses, and a wood-burning stove that bears his name.

Franklin was very involved in Pennsylvania politics and in public service for all the colonies. He played an important role at the Albany Congress during the French and Indian War. He later went to London on behalf of the colonies to protest against British taxation. Franklin then became one of America's key diplomats during the American Revolution.

At 83 years old, Franklin saw George Washington become president under the Constitution that he had helped shape. He died the following year, respected as one of the great men of his time.

young men had fought in the war and been wounded or killed. The colonists thought the British managed their colonies badly, and that they were too proud.

There was another reason colonists did not want to pay any taxes that were for the benefit of Britain. They believed they had no voice in decision-making. This debate, which went on for the next decade, was one of the seeds of the American Revolution. The stage was set for a period in which resentments increased. Revolutionary passions began to simmer.

Common Experiences

New England, the Middle Colonies, and the South grew into very different societies during the 1700s. Yet certain experiences were common to all regions and created bonds of unity among the white settlers.

The French and Indian War, although not fought throughout the colonies, had fostered a common sense of resentment toward Britain. This feeling brought the colonies together.

Another common experience was the growing ability of all white colonists to buy consumer goods. The colonies were deeply involved in trade with Britain. Throughout the century, this trade increased and offered the colonists a wide variety of products that had not been available at the start of the 1700s.

Consumer goods from England and Europe spread through all levels of society. Items previously made in the home or the local community—things such as beds, parlor furniture, china and tableware, clocks, and books—were increasingly imported and sold to colonists. For example, in the New England of 1700, most tables would have been set with spoons made of wood. By the middle of the century, metal knives and forks from Britain were available, and not only to the wealthy. Rich families could afford fine tableware and china imported from Europe. Even poor families could afford less expensive versions of these imports.

This fact created similarities in the way of life across all regions of the colonies. A person who bought an English clock in Massachusetts was much like one who bought the same clock in Virginia. They were both "British" and "colonists" at the same time. They were part of a larger society that had many things in common.

Religious Attitudes

Another thing white British colonists shared was their relationship to religion. As a multicultural society, the colonies had many religions existing side by side. Nearly all white people were Christians. Catholics lived mainly in Maryland, and different forms of Protestantism were spread across the colonies. Puritans, Quakers, Congregationalists, Presbyterians, and Lutherans, were the major sects. There were a few small Jewish communities, the only non-Christian groups among the European settlers.

In spite of this variety of religious faiths, few colonists in the early 1700s went to church. North America's European settlers were seen by outsiders as people who did not care much about religion. Native Americans continued to

> "The truth is, the great Gods of this world are God-belly, God-peace, God-wealth, God-honour, God-pleasure, and God-land."
>
> *Roger Williams, describing the average person's loss of religious zeal*

Jonathan Edwards (1703–58)

Jonathan Edwards fired the flames of religious revival in Massachusetts in the 1730s and 1740s. He gained a wide following because of his powerful sermons.

Edwards was a strict minister who demanded a great deal from his congregation. Some of his followers eventually tired of his preaching. In 1750, Edwards was dismissed from his congregation in Northampton. He moved to Stockbridge, where he took charge of an Indian mission. In 1757, Edwards was appointed president of the College of New Jersey (now Princeton University), but he died before starting the new job.

Edwards is regarded as one of the greatest writers of the colonial period. His sermons are still read today. One of the most famous is *Sinners in the Hands of an Angry God*.

practice their ancient religions, but whites tended to be more wrapped up in their daily lives than in their spiritual welfare. They were busy making a living and getting ahead in life, although they almost always thought of themselves as Christians.

The Great Awakening

In the 1730s, the colonists' attitude began to change again. A series of religious revival movements started, and spiritual feelings became important again. These religious revivals have been called the Great Awakening by historians.

In Massachusetts, the fiery preacher Jonathan Edwards preached Puritan teachings, but did not say that only the chosen few could be saved. Instead, he opened the religion to all comers. His sermons caused people to moan and shriek and collapse as they had religious experiences.

In New Jersey, the preacher William Tennent and his sons claimed miraculous powers as part of their message. Tennent claimed his faith had allowed him to raise his own son from the dead.

One of Britain's most famous preachers, George Whitefield, visited the colonies a number of times during the 1740s. He preached to audiences that numbered in the thousands. Many less well-known imitators also toured the colonies. They carried the message of sin and salvation to remote areas, where people were eager to hear their sermons.

The Great Awakening offered a version of Christianity that promised equality of human beings. This attracted African Americans, and many became Christians in the 1700s. Both white and black people felt they could take control of their spiritual lives by making a decision to reject sin and accept God. The movement spread throughout the colonies, uniting them in another common experience.

The Right to be Different

The Great Awakening that swept over the colonies in the 1700s affected the way people thought about many things. The new emphasis on emotion and feeling was a threat to traditional ministers, who were used to teaching people what they should know about religion.

The Great Awakening was a challenge to authority. People began to believe they had a right to dissent from traditional religion and to be different. In Virginia, for example, the Baptist faith gained a foothold. It challenged the traditional Anglican religion of the wealthy classes. Baptist churches were often racially mixed and were organized along democratic lines. Although some Baptists were slave owners, they were required to treat their slaves fairly and not to break up slave families.

The religious revivals of the 1700s brought many principles and practices of equality into colonial life. These new ideas were to play an important role when the colonists rejected British rule. Even later, the belief in equality and the freedom to be different was important in forming a democratic society in the United States.

Conclusion

Over a period of just 160 years, the British colonies in North America had changed enormously. In the early 1600s, they had been just a handful of tiny English settlements, struggling to survive in a new and sometimes hostile land. By the mid-1700s, there were 13 colonies, comprising large cities, many towns and villages, and a population of over 2.5 million. This figure excludes the Native American people who were there before the white settlers arrived.

As the colonies grew, they acquired a character of their own, separate from their British rulers. But the colonists still thought of themselves as British citizens. This double identity would become increasingly difficult by the 1760s. And in the 1770s, the colonists would be forced to decide if they were British or American. By the end of the 1770s, they had rebelled against the mother country and declared their independence.

How could people who considered themselves British take up arms against their own country? The answer is somewhat complicated. But at the root of the rebellion was a sense that their very rights as British citizens were being trampled on by the government in London. The colonists believed they were being unfairly taxed. They believed that Britain was using the trade and profits of the colonies for its own benefit. They believed they had a right to govern themselves and make the decisions that affected their lives. Taxes, representation, and self-government—all these issues were about to come to a head in the American Revolution.

Glossary

administration   The managing of public affairs or business, or the group of people who carry out the management.

agriculture   The work of farmers, mostly growing crops and raising livestock for food.

allies   Groups of people or countries that side together during a conflict.

authority   The power to make decisions and rules, or the people who have that power.

commerce   The business of buying and selling things.

confederacy   An alliance of several groups that agree to act together and support each other.

congregation   A group of people gathering together, usually to worship.

delegate   The person chosen to represent others at a meeting or in making decisions.

democratic   Describes a system in which people are their own authority rather than being ruled over by a king or queen. In a democratic system, people vote on decisions, or elect representatives to vote for them.

dissenters   People who disagree with the usual ideas and religions in their society.

economics   The production and use of goods and services, and the system of money that is used for the flow of goods and services.

emigrant   A person who leaves his or her home country to go and live somewhere else.

export   To send something abroad to sell or trade. An export is also the thing that is sent, such as tobacco or cotton.

Franciscan   A monk who follows the ideas of St. Francis of Assisi, and who takes a vow of poverty. Franciscans are dedicated to caring for poor or suffering people, and to teaching Christianity.

frontier   The edge of something known or settled. In North America, the frontier for the white settlers moved as they themselves moved west onto new lands.

heresy   A belief that is not allowed or that contradicts the teachings of the church.

immigrant   A person who has left the country of his or her birth and come to live in another country.

migrate	To move from one place to another in search of a new place to live.
militiamen	Members of locally organized military groups.
missionary	A person who goes to another country to convert the people there to his or her religion, and sometimes to help the poor or sick.
multicultural	Made up of more than one culture, such as the mix of Native American, African, and European cultures that existed in colonial America.
outpost	A base in a foreign country or in an outlying area that is used for military defense or for trading.
plantation	A farm where crops, such as tobacco or sugar, are grown and where the work is done by large teams of workers. In the past, these workers were often slaves.
proprietor	The owner or person in charge of a place. Proprietors who received large colonial land grants had the right to govern their land.
Puritans	Members of the Church of England who wanted to reform their church. They became a powerful political force in England during the 1600s.
representation	Having someone to act on behalf of others: to give their views, look after their interests, and to vote for what they want.
revival	When there is a renewed enthusiasm for something in which people had lost interest.
sect	A religious group within a larger religion, such as the many groups within the Christian church.
Separatists	Puritans who wanted to leave the Church of England instead of trying to reform it from within.
stability	A kind of strength that keeps things steady and under control.
strategy	The overall military plan for dealing with an enemy or a conflict.
surveyor	A person whose job it is to measure land, work out boundaries and areas, and make records of the information.
tactics	The moves made in combat to try and defeat an enemy.
trustee	A person who takes charge of land or money or business on behalf of others, and is trusted to act in the best interests of those who benefit from it.

Time Line

1607	English colonists found settlement in Jamestown, Virginia.
1609	Santa Fe, New Mexico, founded.
1616	John Smith publishes map naming New England region.
1619	First Africans arrive in Virginia.
	House of Burgesses founded in Virginia.
1620	Puritans found Plymouth Colony, Massachusetts.
1622	Violent conflict between colonists and Native Americans in Virginia.
1624	Virginia becomes a royal colony.
1626	Dutch West India Company buys Manhattan Island, New York.
1630	John Winthrop leads Puritans to settle Massachusetts Bay Colony.
1632	King Charles I grants Lord Baltimore land for colony in Maryland.
1636	Roger Williams establishes colony in Rhode Island.
1637	Attack on Pequot village by white settlers and Indian allies ends Pequot War.
	Anne Hutchinson excommunicated from church.
1638	New Sweden founded in Delaware Valley.
	Colonists led by Thomas Hooker settle in Connecticut.
1649	Act for Religious Tolerance adopted in Maryland.
1653	First white settlements in North Carolina, at Albemarle Sound.
1663	Carolina proprietors receive charter for Carolina colony.
1664	English seize New Netherland and rename it New York.
1664	Duke of York divides his New York lands and creates colony of New Jersey.
1675–76	Colonists and Indians clash in New England in King Philip's War.
1676	Bacon's Rebellion breaks out in Virginia.
1680	Pueblo Revolt in New Mexico.
	Charleston, South Carolina, founded.
1682	William Penn founds Quaker colony of Pennsylvania.
	René Robert Cavelier, Sieur de La Salle, claims large region of North America for France, and names it Louisiana.
1692	Witch trials in Salem, Massachusetts.
1699	Louisiana region first settled by French.
	Virginia capital moves from Jamestown to Williamsburg.

1702 German emigration to British colonies in North America begins.
      New Jersey becomes a royal colony.
1704 Delaware gets its own assembly, independent of Pennsylvania.
1712 North and South Carolina separate to become two colonies.
1718 New Orleans, Louisiana, founded.
1724 Code Noir adopted in Louisiana.
1733 Colony of Georgia founded.
      Benjamin Franklin begins publishing *Poor Richard's Almanac*.
1734 Religious revival (the Great Awakening) begins in British colonies.
1739 Stono slave rebellion erupts in South Carolina.
1741 Slaves executed in New York.
1754 French and Indian War breaks out.
      Albany Congress meets in Albany, New York.
1755 French Acadians expelled by British from Nova Scotia.
1759 British capture Quebec, capital of New France.
1763 French and Indian War ends with Treaty of Paris.

Further Reading

Bracken, Jean M. *My Life in the American Colonies: Daily Lifestyles of the Early Settlers* (Perspectives on History Series). Carlisle, MA: Discovery Enterprises, 1995.

De Angelis, Therese. *Native Americans and the Spanish* (Indians of North America Series). Broomall, PA: Chelsea House, 1997.

Emert, Phyllis R. *Colonial Triangular Trade: An Economy Based on Human Misery* (Perspectives on History Series). Carlisle, MA: Discovery Enterprises, 1995.

Fradin, Dennis B. *The Maryland Colony* (Thirteen Colonies Series). Danbury, CT: Children's Press, 1990.

Hale, Anna W. *The Mayflower People: Triumphs and Tragedies*. Niwot, CO: Rinehart, Roberts, 1995.

Knight, James E. *Jamestown: New World Adventure* (Adventures in Colonial America Series). Mahwah, NJ: Troll Communications, 1998.

Kroll, Steven. *William Penn: Founder of Pennsylvania*. New York: Holiday House, 1999.

Terkel, Susan L. *Colonial American Medicine* (Colonial America Series). Danbury, CT: Franklin Watts, 1993.

Websites

Monterey County Free Libraries–California Missions – Index to California missions, useful links, and map for locations.
library.monterey.edu/mcfl/mission.html

Slave Narratives – University of Houston. Excerpts from Slave Narratives Edited by Steven Mintz – The Middle Passage.
vi.uh.edu/paages/mintz/primary.htm

Fort Necessity National Battlefield – National Park Service sites related to the French and Indian War.
www.nps.gov/fone/relsites.htm

Bibliography

Axtell, James. *The Invasion Within: The Contest of Cultures in Colonial North America.* New York: Oxford University Press, 1986.

Bailyn, Bernard. *The Peopling of British North America.* New York: Vintage Books, 1988.

Boller, Paul F., Jr., and Ronald Story. *A More Perfect Union: Documents in U.S. History. Vol. 1: To 1877.* New York: Houghton Mifflin, 1991.

Bonomi, Patricia U. *A Factious People: Politics and Society in Colonial New York.* New York: Columbia University Press, 1971.

Boyer, Paul S.; Clifford E. Clark, Jr.; Joseph Kett; Neal Salisbury; Harvard Sitkoff; and Nancy Woloch. *The Enduring Vision: A History of the American People,* second edition. New York: Houghton Mifflin, 1995.

Chestnutt, David R. *South Carolina's Expansion into Colonial Georgia.* New York: Garland, 1989.

Cronon, William. *Changes in the Land: Indians, Colonists, and the Ecology of New England.* New York: Hill and Wang, Inc., 1983.

Ekirch, A. Roger. *Poor Carolina: Politics and Society in Colonial North Carolina, 1729-1776.* Chapel Hill, NC: Univ. of North Carolina Press, 1981.

Hazen-Hammond, Susan. *Timelines of Native American History.* New York: Berkley Publishing Group, 1997.

Innes, Stephen. *Creating the Commonwealth: The Economic Culture of Puritan New England.* New York: W. W. Norton, 1995.

Kulikoff, Alan. *Tobacco and Slaves: The Development of Southern Cultures in the Chesapeake, 1680-1800.* Chapel Hill, NC: Univ. of North Carolina, 1986.

Marcus, Robert D., and Robert Burner. *America Firsthand: Vol. 1: From Settlement to Reconstruction,* second edition. New York: Saint Martin's, 1997.

Rhys, Isaac. *The Transformation of Virginia, 1740-1790.* Chapel Hill, NC: Univ. of North Carolina Press, 1999.

Rutman, Darrett B., and Anita H. Rutman. *A Place in Time: Middlesex County, Virginia, 1650-1750.* New York: W. W. Norton, 1986.

Soderlund, Jean R., ed. *William Penn and the Founding of Pennsylvania, 1680-1684: A Documentary History.* Philadelphia: Univ. of Pennsylvania Press, 1983.

Solow, Barbara, ed. *Slavery and the Rise of the Atlantic System.* New York: Cambridge Univ. Press, 1993.

Index